FREMONT OLDER & THE 1916 SAN FRANCISCO BOMBING

A Tireless Crusade for Justice

JOHN C. RALSTON

THE History PRESS

Published by The History Press
Charleston, SC 29403
www.historypress.net

Copyright © 2013 by John C. Ralston
All rights reserved

Cover images: Front, clockwise from upper left: San Francisco Public Library History Room; author's collection; Bancroft Library; San Francisco Public Library History Room. Back, clockwise from upper left: *San Francisco Chronicle*, July 23, 1916; Bancroft Library; author's photo, mural by Anton Refrigier, Rincon Annex, San Francisco.

First published 2013

Manufactured in the United States

ISBN 978.1.62619.267.6

Library of Congress CIP data applied for.

Notice: The information in this book is true and complete to the best of our knowledge. It is offered without guarantee on the part of the author or The History Press. The author and The History Press disclaim all liability in connection with the use of this book.

All rights reserved. No part of this book may be reproduced or transmitted in any form whatsoever without prior written permission from the publisher except in the case of brief quotations embodied in critical articles and reviews.

Contents

Preface 5
Introduction: "The American Dreyfus Case" 7

San Francisco in 1916 11
War Abroad, War at Home 23
Billings and Mooney 33
Saturday, July 22, 1916: Preparedness Day 41
Arrests 59
Trials 69
The Oxman Letters 91
Billings-Mooney Becomes International 105
The Densmore Report 123
The Cases Drag On and On and On 135
The Newsboy Who Became a Lawyer 159
1939: Free at Last 169

Epilogue 175
Bibliography 183
Index 185
About the Author 191

Preface

This book is the product of a consuming interest in the history of my native city, San Francisco. In particular, it is the product of a long fascination with a figure that dominated my city's history for almost forty years, the great newspaper editor Fremont Older. More about Older's life and career will be found in the first chapter of this work, so it suffices to say here that besides being at the top of his profession, he had a unique gift for personal growth: beginning his career as a yellow journalist who published gossip and scandals in the fashion of the time, he developed into a nonjudgmental figure who looked beneath the surface of individuals and events to seek the root causes of both individual and societal behavior.

In 2003, I gave a presentation to the San Francisco History Association (SFHA) on the Billings-Mooney case that led to a two-part article in the quarterly publication of the San Francisco Museum and Historical Society (SFM&HS) on the case, all of which has culminated in the work you are reading. As so often with anything he touched, Older dominated the case, which unfortunately he did not live to see resolved. While this work may add to the voluminous scholarship on the Billings-Mooney case, I hope that it stands as a tribute to Older and that my writing meets the high standards he demanded of all who worked with and for him.

I would like to thank the staff at the San Francisco Main Library History Room for its help in obtaining photographs and illustrations, as well as permissions to reprint: Jeff Thomas, Dee Dee (Wendy) Kramer, Photo Curator Christina Moretta and Archivist Susan Goldstein. Thanks to

Susan Snyder at the Bancroft Library, University of California–Berkeley, for her prompt help in supplying images and permissions. Thanks also to the unnamed staff at the Green Library, Stanford University, who long ago recognized the guy who keeps coming in requesting obscure old San Francisco newspaper files. Thanks to Paul Middents in Washington State for pointing out today's location of the Alibi Clock that figured so prominently in the Billings-Mooney case. Thanks to Mike, Vince and Josh of the City of Vallejo, California, Department of Public Works, for responding so quickly to my queries about the same clock.

I thank my brother, Stephen, for reading and correcting the section of the epilogue referring to the decisions of the United States Supreme Court under Chief Justice Earl Warren. My special thanks to Aubrie Koenig, commissioning editor at The History Press in Charleston, South Carolina, for her enthusiasm in recognizing the potential of this work and guiding it through publication, and to History Press project editor Ryan Finn.

My final thanks are reserved for a person very special, my wife, Lana. Born in an outlying area of Siberia, a native of the former Soviet Union, she has delved enthusiastically into the history of her adopted state of California. Her contribution to our local Los Altos Hills Historical Society is acknowledged by all who have had the good fortune to experience it. Her contribution to my life is beyond description. This book is dedicated to her.

Introduction

"The American Dreyfus Case"

On Saturday, January 5, 1895, at the École Militaire on Paris's Champs-de-Mars, about 1,200 meters southeast of the looming Eiffel Tower, a strange ceremony was held. In the courtyard, a thirty-six-year-old artillery officer, now a convict, was marched under guard and ordered to halt. As a crowd gawked, another officer ripped off the convict's insignia of rank, buttons and decorations and, in a final degradation, broke his sword over his knee. The humiliated officer was then marched around the courtyard perimeter before soldiers from Paris regiments. Outside the courtyard, it was the crowd's turn. With no such military restraint required of the soldiers in the courtyard, they screamed, "Traitor," "Death to him" and, tellingly, "Dirty Jew!"

The previous September 1894, a cleaning woman at the German embassy, secretly working for France's Statistics (intelligence) Section, had found in a wastebasket a document offering to sell the Germans military secrets. Called the *bordereau*, it appeared to have been written by an officer knowledgeable about French army artillery. Handwriting experts who were shown the document were divided as to who wrote it, but nonetheless, the Statistics Section named a suspect: the degraded artillery officer Captain Alfred Dreyfus. Dreyfus's misfortune was to be in the wrong place at the wrong time. He was Jewish at a time when anti-Semitism was particularly rife in France, which had a long, dishonorable history of it. He was from Alsace, a disputed region on the Franco-German border that was annexed by Germany after France suffered a humiliating defeat in the Franco-Prussian War of 1871. And France's defeat still stung the nation's military establishment. Thus, anti-Semitism, sectionalism and militarism all conspired against Dreyfus. Although his handwriting only slightly matched the writing on the *bordereau*—and another officer's handwriting matched it more—Dreyfus was secretly tried for treason, convicted and sentenced to life in a hellish prison on Devil's Island, just above French Guiana, where he was not expected to live long.

On Saturday, September 23, 1916, more than twenty-one years after Dreyfus's degradation, a jury filed into a San Francisco courtroom after deliberating and announced its verdict: guilty of murder in the first degree. The defendant—now a convicted murderer—was one Warren Knox Billings. The verdict was a shock, so much so that a veteran San Francisco *Bulletin* editor had a heart attack upon hearing it. Oddly, for reasons that would not be revealed for another four years and were questionable even then, prosecuting attorney James Brennan had not asked for the death penalty for Billings but rather life imprisonment. Exultant district attorney Charles M. Fickert said that Billings's conviction was "merely a pioneer case" and that he expected similar verdicts for more defendants.

Less than five months later, on Friday, February 9, 1917, Fickert got his similar verdict. A jury in the murder trial of Thomas ("Tom") J. Mooney also returned a verdict of guilty in the first degree. There was no recommendation of life imprisonment, meaning that Mooney would be sentenced to hang. Tom Mooney's sister, Anna Mooney, screamed and fainted, and his aged mother began crying. Mrs. Israel Weinberg, wife of one of Mooney's codefendants, wailed and fainted as well. Mooney paled but was quiet as he was handcuffed and led from the courtroom. Again, Fickert was jubilant: "We are merely on the threshold of the prosecutions to follow this conviction."

As in the Dreyfus case, there was an indisputable crime. On Saturday, July 22, 1916, a terrorist bomb had exploded during a great patriotic "Preparedness" parade. Ten people were killed and forty injured, many seriously. The murders led to an outcry for arrest and suppression of "anarchists," an umbrella term that included labor figures, nonconformists and other antiestablishment types. Billings was arrested on Thursday the twenty-seventh and Mooney the next day. Both were held incommunicado several days before being booked.

Despite the horrible sentence pronounced on him, Dreyfus was fortunate in one regard, having a close-knit, supportive family of some wealth. In June 1895, his brother, Mathieu, engaged a literary critic to begin a campaign with French authors and intellectuals in proving Alfred Dreyfus's innocence. Belief spread gradually and then grew with revelations of the prosecution's perjury and coverup of the *bordereau*'s real author, Major Ferdinand Esterhazy. To begin with, Dreyfus hadn't a motive for selling secrets to Germany: from a well-off family, with an independent income besides his salary, he didn't need money. Esterhazy meanwhile was a spendthrift and a womanizer and had gambling debts. Support for Dreyfus culminated with the publication in January 1898 of the great French author and journalist Emile Zola's *J'Accuse…!* (I Accuse!), a blistering indictment of Dreyfus's frame-up. *L'Affaire Dreyfus* (the Dreyfus Affair) became international. Outside France, opinion was overwhelmingly favorable to him.

Neither Billings nor Mooney had money, but the American Federation of Labor hired detectives to investigate the chief prosecution witness against Mooney. Acting on a tip, they went to Grayville, Illinois, where they found letters to a local resident indicating that the witness was not even in San Francisco at the time he testified seeing Billings and Mooney plant the bomb. The letters were taken to San Francisco and shown to the great newspaper editor Fremont Older. Older in San Francisco was counterpart to Zola in Paris. He printed the letters on the front page of the evening *Bulletin* and, with others, conducted further investigation that demonstrated that the prosecution's cases against Billings and Mooney were completely fraudulent: prosecution witnesses contradicted themselves and one another; they were paid to testify; the jury foreman in Mooney's trial was in collusion with the district attorney's office. Support for the defendants spread nationally and internationally. Inevitably, Billings-Mooney came to be called "the American Dreyfus Case."

In fact, there were conspicuous parallels. There was an obvious crime, but both prosecutions, rather than investigating to find a suspect or suspects, decided on suspects in advance and then fished for evidence against them. When no evidence was found, the prosecutions faked it. Evidence favoring the defendants was ignored or suppressed. In each case, an institution threatened with exposure closed ranks to protect its own, repeated its discredited cases and attacked its defendants and critics personally rather than admit wrongdoing. The defendants' backgrounds made that easier. For many Frenchmen, Dreyfus's ethnicity was guilt enough, so why bother? The attitude was stated candidly multiple times. Billings and Mooney were societal outcasts. Being suspected of radicalism and of using violence in labor-management disputes earlier, many people said that they deserved imprisonment, guilty of the bombing or not.

There were differences, of course. In France, one man was imprisoned, while in San Francisco, two men were imprisoned and other people tried, but with the prosecution having fallen apart with Fremont Older's exposures of perjury, there were no more convictions. (Most treatments refer to "the Mooney Case," as though it involved just one man, but as there were two, I call it "Billings-Mooney.") And Dreyfus was imprisoned for four and a half years and then retried, pardoned, reinstated in the army and, in 1906, made a Knight of the Legion of Honor in a ceremony in the very courtyard where he had been degraded eleven years earlier. Billings and Mooney were imprisoned far longer, and Billings was not fully exonerated until forty-five years after the Preparedness Day bombing.

Fremont Older and Emile Zola paid dearly for their advocacy. Threats, vituperation, innuendoes and outright lies were used against them. Older almost lost his livelihood at the then advanced age of sixty-two. Zola was tried and convicted of libel because of *J'Accuse…!* and went to England to escape imprisonment. Older was physically attacked, and Zola may even have been murdered, although this was never proven.

France is considered the peak of European civilization, and in many ways it is. The nation has contributed mightily to the visual arts, architecture, design, literature, music, viticulture and cuisine (especially cuisine), and the French are justifiably renowned for knowing how to live well and enjoy life. The Dreyfus Affair, however, exposed fissures in French society. As Zola and his allies (*Dreyfusards*) campaigned for Dreyfus's release, prosecution supporters (*Anti-Dreyfusards*) campaigned to keep an innocent man on Devil's Island rather than compromise the military establishment's "honor." Associates, friends and even families were bitterly divided. The case continues to be much written about. A good recent example is Louis Begley's aptly titled *Why the Dreyfus Affair Matters* (Yale University Press, 2009), a concise treatment of the affair and its relevance today.

In a remarkably short time, California had also become a civilization. After and even during the gold rush, authors, artists, photographers and architects created in new California styles. After the disastrous earthquake and fire of April 1906, San Francisco rose from its ashes and gave the world the Panama-Pacific International Exposition (PPIE) of 1915, to which France had links. Composer Camille Saint-Saëns, France's official representative, composed the piece "Hail, California" for the PPIE, and the French Pavilion inspired a permanent structure, the Legion of Honor Museum. Billings-Mooney, however, also exposed fissures. Some of Fremont Older's earlier allies turned against him. The case was an excuse for capital to suppress labor, which led to the bitter Pacific Coast longshoremen's strike of 1934.

Like the Dreyfus Affair, Billings-Mooney is a seminal case about which every new generation must learn. This is the story of "the American Dreyfus Case."

San Francisco in 1916

In San Francisco, California, in 1916, there began a chain of events that would resound throughout the world, disgracing the city and the United States. Twenty-three years would pass before the disgrace was even partially gone and another twenty-two until it was gone completely. Today, long after the principals have died and the events are mostly forgotten, the Billings-Mooney case is relevant as a demonstration of how civil liberties can be jeopardized when a society reacts to physical danger.

To understand the bitterness of the Billings-Mooney case and why it went on so long, it is necessary to understand San Francisco before the turn of the twentieth century. As everyone knows, San Francisco lies by an active geological fault, the San Andreas. Running down the middle of the city and dividing it roughly in two was another kind of fault, a social, economic and political one that we can call the "Market Street fault." North of Market was mostly middle class and upper-middle class, with the mansions of Nob Hill millionaires—Stanford, Hopkins, Huntington, Crocker, Flood and Towne—dominating all. South of Market—called "South of the Slot" because of the cable car tracks on Market Street that predated the 1906 earthquake and fire—was predominantly working class and transient. "South of the Slot" was more than a geographical expression; it was a way of life.

San Francisco grew in a very short time from a tented town to a major American city, and the demand for skilled workers had almost always exceeded the supply. The city was a union labor stronghold. (Los Angeles by contrast was mostly open shop, and Los Angeles employers were determined to keep it that way.) Management and labor—North of Market and South of Market—clashed regularly in San Francisco, sometimes one side winning, sometimes the other; a war with no decisive battle. In 1901, a bitter teamster-waterfront strike began when business organized the Employers' Association to break union labor. Neither side won a clear victory, but labor men, convinced that neither major political party represented them, organized the Union Labor Party (ULP). The ULP was immediately exploited by a brilliant but unscrupulous lawyer, Abraham Ruef, who engineered the party's nomination for mayor of his friend and client, the tall, handsome, charismatic Eugene E. Schmitz, head of the Musician's Union. Schmitz amazed political authorities by winning easily, although few of the ULP ticket were elected with him.

Ruef's power grab immediately got the notice of Fremont Older, managing editor of the San Francisco evening *Bulletin*. Older, from an impoverished Wisconsin family whose men had been wiped out in the Civil War, was a striking figure, more than six-foot-two and athletic, whose only vice was cigars. Self-educated and a voracious reader, he had learned the newspaper trade from the ground up. He and his brainy, beautiful wife, Cora, a published writer, made a conspicuous and handsome couple in San Francisco. The *Bulletin* was a unique newspaper. Independently owned by Robert A. ("R.A.") Crothers, a Canadian-born lawyer who had inherited it in part from his deceased brother-in-law, Loring Pickering Sr., the paper had a history of crusades against graft and corruption but had deteriorated badly by 1895, when Crothers offered Older the job of managing editor. Feeding readers a mixture of moral zeal and sensationalism, Older boosted *Bulletin* circulation to the largest of any evening newspaper's west of Chicago.

Older had a unique gift for attracting talent: *Bulletin* staff would include cartoonists Rube Goldberg, Robert Ripley (*Ripley's Believe or Not!*) and "Tad" Dorgan and writers and editors Maxwell Anderson (*Key Largo*, *Anne of the Thousand Days*), Robert L. Duffus, Ernest J. Hopkins, Edgar "Scoop" Gleeson and Rose Wilder Lane (who coauthored the *Little House* series, which until recently was attributed solely to her mother, Laura Ingalls Wilder). It was a time when people got all their information from newspapers, and an editor like Older had enormous influence.

After Schmitz was inaugurated in 1902, scraps of information reached Older about graft: payoffs, police overlooking liquor license violation and brothels flourishing with police protection. The *Bulletin* went on the attack, but Schmitz was reelected in 1903. In 1905, Older organized a fusion ticket with Democratic and Republican Parties nominating a single candidate. Mathematically, that seemed sure of winning, but to the horror of Older and his allies, Schmitz won a third term, and the entire Union Labor ticket, including all eighteen members of the board of supervisors, was elected with him.

Shocked by the indifference of San Francisco voters, Older swore to *make* people believe him and went to Washington, D.C., to ask President Theodore Roosevelt to lend a special federal prosecutor, Francis J. Heney, to bring charges against Ruef, Schmitz and the supervisors. Roosevelt eventually agreed to that and also to lending Detective William Burns, but there were obstacles. Costs of the prosecution would be about $100,000, far beyond the district attorney's budget, and the prosecution would have to be conducted under the auspices of District Attorney William Langdon, about whom little was known other than that he had been elected on the ticket chosen by Abraham Ruef.

Older rashly assured Heney and Roosevelt that he would take care of the money, and when he returned to San Francisco, he called on Langdon. Older got a surprise when Langdon assured him that as chief law enforcement officer of San Francisco, he would prosecute *any man* who breaks the law; plainly, that included Ruef. The $100,000 was a problem. Older had no money, but he knew everyone in San Francisco who did, including former mayor James Duvall Phelan and young Rudolph Spreckels, of the Spreckels sugar family, who had made his own fortune and had a strong sense of public duty. Spreckels said that he would back the investigation to the limit, but he and Heney said

The graft prosecution. *Left to right*: Detective Frank Burns, Fremont Older, Cora Older, Francis Heney, Charles Cobb and Rudolph Spreckels. *Bancroft Library*.

that prosecution must not be limited to a few corrupt officials—it had to go to the very top, including the officials of the Southern Pacific railroad, which had corrupted California and debauched government.

The graft prosecution began early in 1906 and was kept secret at first. The destruction of San Francisco in the earthquake and fire was a setback to the prosecution: Schmitz rose to the occasion and, rightly or wrongly, was hailed a hero, but in October 1906, the graft prosecution went public. Ruef uncharacteristically panicked and tried to have Langdon removed as district attorney but lost the fight in court. The prosecution set a trap for the supervisors. They fell into it and confessed to taking money in Ruef's bribery schemes. Ruef and Schmitz were indicted by a new grand jury, and Ruef eventually changed his plea to an extortion charge from not guilty to guilty. In May 1907, Mayor Schmitz was convicted of extortion and was sentenced by Judge Frank Dunne to five years' imprisonment.

San Francisco was behind the graft prosecution until Heney began to do what he had promised and sought indictments against wealthy and prominent members of society who had collaborated with Ruef. In May 1907, the Car Men's Union began a bitter, violent strike against the United Railways (URR), which ran San Francisco's streetcars. The *Bulletin* charged that Patrick Calhoun, the company president who had been indicted for passing $200,000 to Ruef and the supervisors to have them vote for an overhead trolley franchise, had engineered the strike to create sympathy for himself. San Francisco was rebuilding from the fire of April 1906, and the last thing people wanted was delay. Calhoun exploited the situation: fights broke out between strikers and strikebreakers, and Calhoun rode up and down Market Street in an open car during the strike and was hailed a hero. "There's a man who isn't afraid of anything," Older heard people say. "He'll break this strike if anyone can." The strike was crushed, and the union was broken. When Older asked a prominent man if he didn't want to see Calhoun convicted if he were guilty of bribing the supervisors, the man said, "If I were on the jury I'd vote to acquit him if he were guilty as hell! He's the man who saved San Francisco."

The novelist Gertrude Atherton expressed the feelings of upper-class San Francisco when she said:

> *The bringing of Calhoun to trial was the signal for a disruption of society rivaling that caused by the Civil War…The wives were as vehement in his support as their husbands. Mrs. Spreckels…suddenly found herself an outsider. So did Mrs. Heney, who was a member of one of the older*

Southern families…One wife of [an accused] *millionaire…went so far as to demand the politics of her guests as they crossed her threshold. And among all there was a bitterness unspeakable.*

Ostracism was not all that the graft prosecution had to endure. Fremont Older was arrested on Van Ness Avenue by two Los Angeles deputies who showed a warrant for his arrest for libel, and he was hustled on board a southbound train at gunpoint. The plot was to take him off and murder him, but an anonymous tipster heard the kidnappers say something about giving Older "a run through the mountains" and called Older's friends in San Francisco. Francis Heney was shot in court (not fatally) by a prospective juror whose criminal past Heney had exposed. In 1907, however, San Francisco elected as mayor Dr. Edward Robeson Taylor, who had replaced Schmitz, and Langdon was reelected with him. The graft prosecution continued until the 1909 election, when Langdon and Taylor did not run again.

Heney ran for district attorney. The graft defendants tried another tactic: they ran their own candidate for district attorney, a Stanford University alumnus named Charles M. Fickert. Fickert had a hard time fitting in at Stanford. He was a country boy from Tehachapi and was snubbed until his second year, when he tried out for the football team. More than six-foot-two and two hundred pounds, he became one of the best linemen in the country. He read law, was admitted to the bar and married the daughter of a Southern Pacific official. His career drifted until James Brennan, a Stanford

Fickert the football star, carried by graft defendants and politicians. *From the* Bulletin, *October 27, 1909.*

classmate, suggested that he run for office. *Bulletin* writer Ernest Jerome Hopkins noted, "Fickert was a lawyer of no discernible ability, prompted and advised at every major turn by lawyers of the 'open shop' group…His best friends never called him brilliant."

Fickert's primary campaign spent $5,000 and deployed a small army of precinct workers. "Fickert is a poor man, and this is not his money," noted the *Bulletin*. "Who is spending nearly five thousand dollars?" Fickert was nominated by the odd combination of Republican and Union Labor Parties, and his November campaign was full of fantastic charges, delivered faster than Heney could respond to them: the prosecutors were themselves grafters; Heney was "the biggest faker and demagogue in existence"; and Heney had taken bribes from Spreckels and had gotten the Democratic nomination by fraud. Hiram Johnson, who prosecuted Ruef after Heney was shot, said, "Fickert has run riot with lies. I think he's gone stark, raving mad…The miserable poltroon wants office so badly that he'll sell his soul to get it." Heney said what he thought of Fickert for accepting the support of men who, if elected, he would be bound to prosecute. But Fickert won. To Older and his allies, it was an indication of how unpopular the graft prosecution had become.

Fickert drank heavily, put words in other people's mouths and threatened to get physical with anyone who disagreed with him, but he fulfilled his backers' expectations, moving to dismiss some indictments and prosecuting others so lackadaisically that acquittal was inevitable.

Charles M. Fickert, circa 1910. *Library of Congress*.

The graft prosecution was over, but it had positive results. Two journalists, Chester Rowell and Edward Dickson, disgusted with the corruption of the 1907 legislature, organized the Lincoln-Roosevelt League of Progressive Republicans, and Older persuaded Hiram Johnson to run for governor as a Progressive in 1910. The Progressives had pushed a direct primary law through the legislature, and Johnson won the Republican nomination in the first primary election in California's history.

Johnson campaigned all over the state by automobile, promising to "Kick the Southern Pacific Railroad out of politics," and was elected governor. His administration installed a new state railroad commission; passed the initiative, referendum and recall; and gave women the vote.

Older had an epiphany. When Ruef's last appeal failed and he went to San Quentin in 1911, Older felt ashamed for having believed in sending just one man to jail without changing the system. He astounded both friends and enemies by visiting Ruef in San Quentin and asking his forgiveness. The *Bulletin* published Ruef's memoirs, and Older campaigned for Ruef's parole, which was not granted until 1915. Older's seeming conversion astounded friend and enemy alike. In a letter to Dr. S.W. Hopkins of Lodi, California, referring to an earlier piece by him in the journal *The Survey*, he explained his reasoning:

> *If you read my article in The Survey, I think there is much in it that you did not understand. Perhaps I did not make myself clear. I tried to. I wanted those who read the Survey article to believe that I at least no longer think we are going to better the world by punishing men individually. I do not feel that it is good for people…to want vengeance administered to our brothers and sisters. I think vengeance, and by vengeance I mean punishment, makes us all worse rather than better. I have asked for mercy for Ruef because I felt that I, above all others, had done most to bring about his downfall. If you have followed the long the fight* The Bulletin *has made during the past eight or nine years, you will recall that I was fighting Ruef long years before the city woke up. You will also recall that I attacked him bitterly with all the invectives that I could personally command, and all that I could hire. I cartooned him in stripes. I described him on his way to San Quentin; told how I thought he would act en route, and what his manner would be when the barber shaved his head, and how he would feel when locked up in a cell. I was vindictive, unscrupulous, savage. I went to Washington and enlisted Heney in the fight. Burns came, and Spreckels joined in the chase. Then I pursued with the same relentless spirit in the wake of these men. At last, after eight years of a man-hunting and man-hating debauch, Ruef crossed over and became what I had wanted him to be, what I had long and dreamed that he might be—a convict, stripped of his citizenship, stripped of everything society values except the remnant of an ill-gotten fortune. It was then I said to myself: "I have got him. He is in stripes. He is in a cell. His head is shaved. He is in tears. He is helpless, beaten, chained—killed, so far as his old life is concerned. You have won. How do you like your*

victory? You painted it. Every savage instinct in your nature is expressed on the canvas."

My soul revolted. I thought over my own life and the many unworthy things I had done to others, the injustice, the wrongs I had been guilty of, the human hearts I had wantonly hurt, the sorrow I had caused, the half-truths I had told, and the mitigating truths I had withheld, the lies I had allowed to go undenied. And then I saw myself also stripped, that is, stripped of all pretense, shame, self-righteousness, holding the key to another man's cell. I dropped the key. I never want to see it again. Let it be taken up and held by those who feel they are justified in holding it. I want no more jail keys. For the rest of my life I want to get a little nearer to the forgiving spirit that Christ expressed.

Isn't what I am accusing myself of, true of all of us? Think it over. Think of your own life. Think of the lives of those around you, and see if you cannot discern that we are all guilty. And then think whether or not you believe that society will be benefited by denying Ruef a parole, which only gives him a half liberty and still holds him under the restrictions of the prison until his term is finished.

In 1914, the Olders bought a fruit ranch about a mile and a half above Cupertino, California, and built a house that they named Woodhills. The house, in a natural bowl about a mile and a half up twisty Prospect Road, is a uniquely livable design by San Jose architects Wolfe and Wolfe, with possible input by

Woodhills, the Olders' home, seen from the south just after completion, circa 1916. *Mort and Elaine Levine.*

Cora. It is L-shaped, with the long axis of the "L" in front. A staircase leads right to a broad porch facing downhill. To the left, an exterior brick staircase under a pergola rises to a garden enclosed by the "L," where the Olders and guests took their ease. On the right, the base of the "L" had bedrooms, with a narrow staircase leading to a cupola, a hideaway where Cora wrote. Woodhills' location required Older to rise early to take a commute train to San Francisco, but the house was a restorative, a refuge to which Older looked forward to returning in the evenings as the sun set behind the hills to the west.

At Woodhills, the Olders entertained *Bulletin* staff, artists, politicians and authors. Visitors over the years included Carl Sandburg, Lincoln Steffens and Clarence Darrow, among other famous names. *Bulletin* editorial writer Robert L. Duffus wrote later that all significant visitors to San Francisco were detoured to the Olders' ranch. The Olders were also host to a raffish crowd of criminals and others whom Older would try to reform, with little success. At the *Bulletin*, 767 Market Street, his cluttered, cigar-littered office was open to everyone. A soft touch, he gave away too much money until his attorney and Cora put him on an allowance. To thousands of San Franciscans, he was "Father Confessor to a City" and their best friend. Others thought him the most dangerous man in San Francisco.

In 1911, San Francisco elected as mayor James Rolph Jr. ("Sunny Jim"). Jim was the cure after the tragedy of the earthquake, the fire and the bitterness of the graft prosecution—the perennial optimist, always smiling, always with a handshake. Sunny Jim was everywhere. He greeted dignitaries, cut ribbons, inaugurated streetcar lines, led parades and threw out baseball season's first ball. He was a businessman, but he was from South of Market, with a foot in both camps. Rolph has been called all style, but his administration accomplished more in San Francisco than any since.

James ("Sunny Jim") Rolph Jr., circa 1910. *Author's collection.*

Ever since the earthquake and fire of 1906 had shaken city hall apart, San Francisco had been without one. Before taking office,

Panama-Pacific International Exposition (PPIE), 1915. The Tower of Jewels is at left. *Author's collection.*

Rolph assembled a board of architects to submit proposals for a new building. In March 1912, a construction bond issue passed overwhelmingly. A design competition was held, the winner being the firm of Bakewell and Brown, whose design was one of the finest examples of French High Baroque Revival anywhere in the world. Ground was broken in 1913, and Rolph presided at the building's dedication in December 1915. Exposition Auditorium on Grove Street was dedicated, by Sunny Jim naturally, in January 1915, and in the same year, ground was broken for a new Main Library in the same civic center complex. Prior to the construction of the new civic center was another seminal event. On December 28, 1912, ten new electric streetcars of the A line rolled east out of a new car barn on Geary Street. The line was a double history maker: the first public street railway not only in San Francisco but also the United States. At Geary and Kearny Streets, Sunny Jim stepped aboard the first car, paying the five-cent fare with the first nickel stamped at the United States Mint on Fifth Street.

The crown jewel of Rolph's administration was the Panama-Pacific International Exposition (PPIE), celebrating the opening of the Panama

Canal and San Francisco's recovery from the earthquake and fire. Ten main exhibit palaces occupied a rectangle roughly one mile long in today's Marina District, with a series of courtyards. At the eastern end of the main block was the Palace of Machinery, almost one thousand feet long, so cavernous that aviator Lincoln Beachey flew through it before its completion. At the western end was architect Bernard Maybeck's Palace of Fine Arts, a haunting evocation of classical antiquity. When the PPIE opened on February 20, 1915, Sunny Jim Rolph, of course, led a grand procession down Van Ness Avenue to the gates, so excited he ran the whole way. The PPIE was a resounding success, attracting 18 million visitors from February to December 1915.

Rolph would be elected mayor five times, serving nineteen years, longer than any mayor before or since, until he was elected governor of California in 1930. He should, however, have quit after two terms while he was still ahead.

War Abroad, War at Home

World War I was the result of what George Washington had called "entangling alliances," against which he had warned upon leaving the presidency. The German Reich, Bismarck's recent creation, allied with the Austro-Hungarian empire. France and Russia, ancient enemies of Germany, were joined by Britain, suspicious of Germany's economic resurgence and growing navy. All powers were bound to back their allies in any dispute, even a minor one, practically guaranteeing general war.

On June 28, 1914, a crazed individual struck a match to the European powder keg. Austria-Hungary had bottled up Serbian access to the Adriatic Sea by sponsoring an artificial Kingdom of Albania, infuriating Serbia and its Slavic ally, Russia. Archduke Franz Ferdinand, heir to the Austro-Hungarian throne, and his wife, paying a state visit to Sarajevo, then part of the Austro-Hungarian empire, were shot dead in an open car by a Serbian member of the terrorist group Black Hand. Austria, with German backing, made retaliatory demands on Serbia. Serbia, with Russian backing, resisted. France backed Russia. When Serbia resisted a crucial item of Austria's ultimatum, Austria declared war. Russia mobilized against both Germany and Austria. Germany declared war on Russia and then on France; when the German army crossed Belgium on its way to France, Britain declared war on Germany.

Incapable of preventing war, the European powers were equally incompetent in fighting it. Germany, planning to crush France in a few weeks, threw seventy-eight divisions across its borders above Switzerland

Death gloats as Europe marches to war. *From the* Bulletin, *August 6, 1914.*

against eighty-three Allied divisions, but when attacked by Russia in the east, it withdrew crucial forces from the Western Front. A colossal, stalemated war of position began. One side would throw thousands of men against entrenched enemy forces with only minimal gains; the other side would counterattack days or weeks later, sometimes regaining territory, sometimes not. Both sides suffered unprecedented casualties: "Twenty million men are patiently trying to outmurder each other," said a *Bulletin* editorial. More than

8 million men and women would die, and many who survived went home maimed, gassed or driven out of their minds.

Europe, which had dominated the world financially, was squandering resources as well as men. In London on April 4, 1916, Chancellor of the Exchequer Reginald McKenna staggered the House of Commons by announcing in his budget speech that the national debt had nearly tripled since the war began and that the war was costing the equivalent of $25 million *per day*! One month later, the Mechanics and Metals National Bank of New York published a booklet noting that the combined cost of the war among all the belligerents was $91 million per day, with no end in sight.

The day after Germany launched its offensive on the Western Front, a *Bulletin* editorial by Duffus ("A War Which Will Have No Winner") noted:

> *Across the Atlantic Ocean the wheel of time has spun backward, and Europe has slipped into temporary barbarism. Every constructive business and occupation, by which nations live and progress, has been thrust into an inferior position by the business of killing, destroying, and laying waste. The armies of Europe are madly at work tearing down society.*
>
> *Just why this must be nobody has said. The diplomatic reasons given are satisfactory, so far as the diplomats are concerned. They explain why kings and emperors wanted war. They do not explain why whole nations are willing to follow kings and emperors into war…No emperors or kings or very high army officers will be killed in battle in this war. Those who will be killed and wounded will be mostly workingmen and workingmen's children. The property of workingmen—the small farmers—will be ravaged and stolen. Workingmen, after the war, will pay for the war in heavy taxes, high prices and low wages. It will take them decades to get it paid for…*
>
> *No gains, even to the winners, will be more than a drop in the bucket in comparison with the costs. War is an absurd investment, even for the trading class, and conquered territory is merely a form of insurance against peace.*

Turmoil extended beyond the European continent. In Dublin, Ireland, the Easter Rising against British rule began in April 1916 when insurgent leader Pádraic Pearse proclaimed an Irish Republic on the steps of the General Post Office after the rebels seized it as their headquarters. British authorities suppressed the rebellion, tried fourteen rebels before summary military tribunals and shot them. German agents had fomented discontent in Ireland and had supplied arms to Sir Roger Casement, who had served in the British Consular Service and was famous for exposing barbaric treatment of indigenous peoples by colonial powers in Africa and Latin America. Casement was put on shore in Ireland by a German submarine but was caught, tried for treason and hanged in London. The executions were a blow to British prestige, especially in cities such as San Francisco, with large populations (and officeholders) of Irish birth or descent.

Closer to home was revolution in Mexico, which American and other foreign investors had treated as their fiefdom. Such names as Guggenheim, U.S. Steel, Anaconda and, conspicuously, Phoebe Apperson Hearst and her son, William Randolph, owned mines, oil fields, cattle ranches and sugar and coffee plantations, exploiting Mexico's natural wealth while openly expressing contempt for its people. By 1916, after the ouster of dictator Porfirio Díaz and the murder of his successor, Francisco Madero, by General Victoriano Huerta, Mexico was divided and unstable under the new government of Venustiano Carranza.

In January, guerrilla leader Francisco ("Pancho") Villa, possibly because of resentment against Americans for cutting off his arms shipments and supporting Carranza, stopped a train full of American mining engineers in Chihuahua and murdered fifteen of them. In April, several hundred *Villastas* crossed the border into Columbus, New Mexico, and killed seventeen Americans. Woodrow Wilson ordered General John Pershing to cross the Mexican border and capture Villa, but the wily guerrilla leader evaded Pershing. Carranza and most Latin Americans saw Pershing's incursion as an act of war, and it aroused fierce resentment among Latin American émigrés and sympathizers in San Francisco. American troops and Mexican regulars clashed at Carrizal, but to Wilson's credit, he stopped short of war and sent a peace commission to Mexico, one member of which was David Starr Jordan of Stanford.

The Hearst press, which had begun in San Francisco with William Randolph's acquisition of his flagship paper the *Examiner*, fairly screamed for forcible annexation of Mexico and the civilization of its "mongrel mixture of Aztec, Indian, and Spanish buccaneer" population:

> *Our army should go forward into Mexico—first to rescue Americans, and secondly to redeem Mexicans.*
>
> *Our flag should wave over Mexico as the symbol of the rehabilitation of that unhappy country and its redemption to "humanity" and civilization.*
>
> *…If we have no right in Mexico we have no right in California or in Texas, which we redeemed from Mexico.*

If we have no right in Mexico we have no right anywhere in the U.S., for this whole country from ocean to ocean, has been rescued from savagery and redeemed for civilization.

...And what we conquer let us conserve for the advantage and advancement of all mankind.

The *Bulletin* took a different view:

If Mexico ever comes under the control of the United States one thing will surely happen. Mexico will be managed first for the interests of Americans and only secondly for the interests of Mexicans. This will make a Mexican democracy impossible. The United States government will be an empire in Mexico and a democracy only on the northern shores of the Rio Grande. But a government is not likely to endure half imperialism and half democracy, any more than half free and half slave. Consequently, since democracy in Mexico will not be congenial to Mexico the final result is likely to be the decline of democracy in the United States. It may not be spectacular, but it will happen...The United States will choke out a promising economic movement in Mexico, and kill its own liberalism.

Annexation is a nightmare—not likely to be seen in broad daylight. Still, it is better not to be fooled by the foolish or dishonest arguments that are constantly being made in its favor.

In his editorial on the outbreak of World War I, Duffus wrote that "Europe is just a San Francisco on a large scale, with its different nationalities living in restricted districts instead of scattering themselves more or less freely." Put the other way, San Francisco was the world in microcosm. The spirit of civic unity that produced the Exposition had dissipated, and San Francisco was back to its old self.

Particularly divisive nationally and locally was "Preparedness," an ostensibly patriotic movement for American involvement in war in Europe, Mexico, the Pacific or all three. The United States under the Wilson administration was neutral in Europe, but pro-ally, anti-German sentiment was high. As the war dragged on, Preparedness agitation increased. Nationally and in San Francisco, Preparedness was supported almost entirely by capitalists and the right. Labor and the left denounced it as a plot for businessmen to stir up support for fat government contracts for arms, warships and other materiel. Preparedness rallies were countered by anti-

Preparedness rallies. One of the latter was held on Monday, July 17, 1916, in Idora Park, Oakland, where a Methodist minister, Reverend John M. Jackson, denounced Preparedness as "this terrible aberration of preparanoia. All over the country in the largest cities men and women are being stampeded in great crowds like frightened cattle, and certain interested parties are at work stampeding them as hard as they can. These interested parties are trying to stampede the whole nation. Why are they doing it? Because they want money." Labor was also suspicious of enlarging the military, which had been used domestically for bloody and unwarranted suppression of strikes and other labor discord.

Ernest Hopkins wrote:

> *No one was or could be quite sane. The thing was driving us into verbalism, into large groupings of factions, so that bankers and munitions-makers and militarists and temperamental fighters were promulgating one definition of patriotism, and liberals and laborites and religionists and Wilsonians were promulgating a very different definition of patriotism.*

The most prominent anti-Preparedness leaders in San Francisco were Rudolph Spreckels and Fremont Older. The *Bulletin* regularly printed attacks on Preparedness by clergy, academics and social critics. Naturally, many readers took exception to its stance. One wrote to Older asking, "Will you state on your editorial page your conviction that this country will never be invaded, [and] that no further preparations for national defense are needed?" To which Older replied:

> *The editor of* The Bulletin *is not convinced that this country will never be invaded. He doesn't know. He thinks not. If a majority of his countrymen will feel more comfortable with long-range coast defense guns, submarines, mines and other apparatus not easily used for any purpose other than defense, he does not see why they should not have them. He would regard such arming less as an insurance against war than as an insurance against nervousness. He knows, however, and his questioner must know, that the current movement for preparedness is not wholly a movement for defense...The editor of* The Bulletin *gravely suspects that many militarists are not entirely frank in this respect. He suspects that many of those who try to frighten the public with lurid prophecies of invasion are perfectly well aware that invasion is unlikely if not entirely impossible, and actually yearn to make this government*

> *an offensive military and naval power. In this ambition he is unable to discern either democracy, virtue, or necessity.*
>
> *The editor of* The Bulletin *finds many dangers which seem to him far more serious than the danger of invasion. Militarism is only one of them. He would like to see his country prepared against avoidable poverty, against industrial tyranny, against unemployment, against legalized injustice, against false standards arising from the unmanly worship of wealth and power.*

Supporters and opponents of the graft prosecution of 1905–9 divided almost evenly on Preparedness: Older's prosecution allies were mostly anti-Preparedness. His opponents, many of them wealthy capitalists who had been indicted, backed it almost to a man. San Francisco's own Preparedness parade was scheduled for Saturday, July 22, 1916. Adding to the divisiveness, the chief organizer and grand marshal was Thornwell Mullally, son-in-law of Patrick Calhoun, the most conspicuous businessman-defendant in the graft prosecution.

There were, however, realignments. Former mayor James Phelan, elected United States senator in 1914, unsuccessfully proposed a $10 million naval and aviation academy to be located in California and successfully pushed for an allocation of $500,000 to expand Mare Island Naval Shipyard. Lawyer and former *Bulletin* editorial writer Eustace Cullinan wrote to Older an open letter listing five areas in which he said the paper had misunderstood or misrepresented Preparedness: war, social justice, security, self-defense and militarism. The *Bulletin* graciously acknowledged Cullinan's conception of a Preparedness that was intellectually and ethically worthy of respect but denied that it had accused all Preparedness advocates of wanting war and denied that Preparedness guaranteed security: "Germany was the best prepared nation on earth, and Germany is bleeding to death." With remarkable prescience, the *Bulletin* advocated an international body to enforce peace, as would the charter of the United Nations in 1945: "Whatever else we do there will be no security until a world police force takes the place of competitive national security." Regarding social justice, the *Bulletin* conceded that many Preparedness advocates wanted it, but as so often happens in wartime, social justice would be put on a back burner. As to what constituted an adequate domestic defense, it quoted Assistant Secretary of the Navy Franklin D. Roosevelt, among others, as saying that the necessary preparedness already existed.

The most conspicuous former ally of Older turned war hawk was Theodore Roosevelt, who by 1916 had become, said Duffus, "something we scarcely recognized," a militarist who derided effeminate "peace prattlers" and who was turning right domestically. A *Bulletin* editorial noted:

> *Peace advocates ought not to make Colonel Roosevelt's mistake and make unkind remarks about him. Most men can remember when they thought exactly as Colonel Roosevelt does about war. All boys who are worth their salt want to be Indians, pirates, bandits, and soldiers. All boys who are boys play at fighting. Most boys like to punch each other's faces. Sometimes the liking lasts over in mature life, but generally, with many other traits of varying ethical value, it is lost. The trouble with Colonel Roosevelt is that he never did lose his boyish pugnacity. He wouldn't grow up.*

San Francisco was considered the strongest union city in the country, which business openly resented. "Is union labor really holding back the growth of San Francisco?" asked the chamber of commerce rhetorically. "Have we a union labor oligarchy which has driven many industries from our city and is keeping many others from coming?" In June 1916, the International Longshoremen's Association struck over wages, breaking its contract with waterfront employers. After a temporary truce, the strike resumed. Two longshoremen were killed in fights with strikebreakers in Oakland and San Francisco; it was the bitterest strike since 1901.

On June 21, the chamber issued a declaration that essentially called for the resumption of the open (nonunion) shop. The *Bulletin* called this a "declaration of war which may cause endless loss and suffering, yet which cannot result in a settlement of the labor problem…Union men know of but two kinds of 'shops'—the union shop and the non-union shop. At the present stage of industry either the workingman has a powerful voice in shop control or he has no voice at all; there is no middle stage. A fight for the 'open shop' is a fight against unionism. If the members of the Chamber of Commerce want to return to the conditions which prevailed when labor was entirely unorganized they should say so."

On July 10, more than one thousand chamber businessmen met at the Merchants' Exchange Building to hear chamber president Frederick Koster deplore the "intolerable condition on the waterfront"—manifestation, he said, of a "disease permeating the community." The chamber's June declaration, rather than being reconsidered, was cheered. Captain Robert Dollar of the Dollar Steamship Lines recalled that waterfront peace had been established during a former strike by sending several ambulance loads of union men to the emergency hospitals: "I want to tell the managers of this movement that that is the way to establish peace and quiet." The chamber appointed a subcommittee, the Law and Order Committee, with five members and Koster as president, to enforce "the right to employ union men in whole or in part as the parties involved may elect"; $200,000 was immediately pledged to the open shop fight, and the figure would climb to $600,000. (Disclosure: The author's grandfather Henry J. "Harry" Ralston Sr., a San Francisco businessman, was a member of the Law and Order Committee.)

Open shop advocates maintained that they were acting in the workers' best interests as well as their own, defending workingmen who wished to work without a union. To union labor, this was hypocrisy, just a cover for business's ultimate aim to break unions or weaken them to the point that workingmen would be helpless. Many businessmen gave that impression. When Republican presidential candidate Charles Evans Hughes campaigned in San Francisco in July, his managers, among other blunders that may have cost Hughes California and the presidency, scheduled a luncheon at the Commercial Club, which flaunted an open shop placard in its window. A strike against the Commercial Club by three culinary unions being imminent, Hughes's manager, Charles Farnham, tried to arrange a compromise with Hugo Ernst of the Cooks and Waiters Union to delay the strike until after Hughes left, to avoid alienating labor voters. Ernst agreed on condition that the placard come down, but when Farnham asked a prominent Republican politician to agree to the deal, he was told, "Take down those placards? Not on your life. We've got those labor bastards in this town where we want them at last, and we are not going to let up on them at all."

San Francisco having a gift for drawing attention to itself, the open shop campaign and the Law and Order Committee was watched nationally. In *The Survey* for November 26, 1916, journalist Harry F. Grady wrote:

> *The weakness of the position of the Chamber of Commerce lies in the fact that its move is not disinterested, as its leaders would have you believe. Whatever sentiments the employer may express about the welfare of the worker, there is always implied a welfare which does not encroach upon profits, or his complete control of his business. He fears the power of organized labor and resents the demands which it makes. Concessions of wages and hours are as nothing to enforce those demands which labor has shown. Hence, the San Francisco Chamber of Commerce will theoretically*

> *concede anything in the matter of improved conditions for labor, if only labor will not show its teeth and fight.*

"Law and order" was code for suppressing labor. In a rejoinder to a later *Survey* article by San Francisco Chamber of Commerce vice-president Robert Newton Lynch, Grady wrote, "No one can deny the right of the Chamber of Commerce to oppose the closed [union] shop…But the closed shop is just as legal as the open shop and a law-and-order campaign has no relevancy whatsoever to such an issue."

With everything happening in San Francisco—reminders of the graft prosecution, strikes, the open shop drive, war in Europe, the execution of Irish patriots, Preparedness, Pershing's incursion in Mexico and more—the stage was set for the reopening of old wounds and the opening of some new ones. The *Bulletin* was not immune. Crothers's nephew, Loring Pickering Jr., who would inherit the paper, was taking charge. Pickering Jr. was his uncle's nephew in the sense that he wanted a paper that reflected his tastes and his desire to be liked by the right people. Like Crothers, Pickering feared losing advertising, and with Crothers's tacit approval, Pickering Jr. was going over Older's head, rescinding orders, killing editorials and scrapping or changing stories he thought might offend businessmen. As Duffus observed, Pickering did not see that a newspaper was not just a building and equipment. The *Bulletin* had a soul, which was embodied by Older. By catering to what he thought the advertisers wanted, Pickering risked losing that soul and making the paper what it had never been: dull.

The strain on Older was not obvious at first. The staff had made a god of him, an "indomitable force," said Duffus, indefatigable and undefeatable. But Older was taking the evening train to Woodhills in despair and humiliation. He had a mortgage and could not guess what would become of him and Cora if he were forced out of the *Bulletin* at age sixty. He ate little dinner, and afterward, he walked down to sit under an oak tree with his dogs and stroke them.

Billings and Mooney

Early in July 1916, Duffus went to the office of *Bulletin* labor editor Fred Ely and found that Ely had company, a man about five-foot-ten, about 190 pounds, with a stocky build, a chubby face, dark hair, dark eyes and thick dark eyebrows that accentuated the man's intense expression. The man was Thomas Jeremiah ("Tom") Mooney. Born in Chicago in 1882 to an Irish American father and Irish mother from County Mayo, Tom had been baptized Catholic and attended Catholic school, but after being thrashed by a priest who accused him of lying, he transferred himself to a public one and broke with the church. It was the earliest manifestation of a rebellious quality that he would display his whole life. Tom's father, Bernard (or Bryan?), a miner who was often blacklisted for union activities, died of "miner's con" (silicosis) when Tom was ten. Mother Mary went to work sorting rags in a paper mill in Holyoke, Massachusetts, for sixty hours per week for four dollars. Tom was apprenticed as an iron molder at age fifteen, and when he was twenty, he joined a union that merged with the International Molders.

Tom Mooney went from place to place, geographically and intellectually. He was frequently laid off or disciplined for union activities, and in 1907, with money saved from several years' work, he toured Europe. He toyed with the idea of becoming an artist after seeing European museums, but while gazing at a Rembrandt in Rotterdam, he met an American socialist named Nicholas Klein who had just returned from an international socialist meeting in Stuttgart. Klein saw Mooney's union pin, they had an intense conversation and

Tom Mooney as an employee at the PPIE, 1915. *Donna Ewald Huggins.*

Rena Mooney, circa 1915. *From* The Survey, *July 7, 1917.*

Mooney returned to the United States a committed socialist and avid reader of socialist literature.

The Panic of 1907 had set in, and work was almost nonexistent in Mooney's trade, which confirmed his socialist beliefs. He drifted cross-country, working at odd jobs until he found a molder's job in Stockton, California. There he met Rena Hermann, a young pianist and piano teacher who had married a semi-invalid, possibly as much out of pity as love. Tom and Rena struck sparks immediately, Rena asked her husband for a divorce, to which he agreed, and she began proceedings. Rena had opened her own teaching studio in San Francisco, but it was wiped out in the earthquake and fire of April 1906, and she prepared another pending her divorce and remarriage.

In 1908, when socialist presidential candidate Eugene V. Debs whistle-stop campaigned in Stockton on his train, the "Red Special," Tom hawked socialist literature so effectively that Debs noticed him. It began a reputation that would help, and harm, Mooney. Shortly afterward, he entered a contest soliciting subscriptions to the socialist journal *Wilshire's Monthly*—financed, ironically, by the Southern California realtor after whom Wilshire Boulevard in Los Angeles is named—and ran such a close second that he won an all-expenses-paid trip to the International Socialist Congress in Copenhagen. Taking his brother, John, who with mother Mary had moved to San Francisco, Mooney met among others the Russian delegate Vladimir Ilyich Ulyanov, better known as "Lenin."

Coming to San Francisco in 1910, Mooney joined the International Workers of the World (IWW, or "the Wobblies"). Tom and Rena were married, and she opened a studio in the Eilers Building, where pianos and other instruments were sold, at 975 Market Street on the south side of the block between Fifth and Sixth Streets. When her teaching day ended—she was reputedly quite a good teacher—she typed letters, solicited subscriptions to *Wilshire's* and opened her studio to socialists and other left-wingers for meetings. Tom left the IWW after three months, joined a radical faction of the Socialist Party and ran for municipal offices. Although unsuccessful as an office-seeker, he more than succeeded at drawing attention to himself. *Bulletin* staffer Ernest Hopkins, covering a 1911 Socialist Party convention, found Mooney "the lusty-voiced, aggressive, belligerent spokesman of the Socialist left-wing":

> *Socialists, then as now, lived by resolutions; in this convention, whenever a resolution of policy was offered that savored of* [gradualism], *it was Mooney who would leap to his feet, and oppose, sometimes flushing with his own oratory.*
>
> *...This bold agitator was...ambitious, belligerent, angrily eloquent, a stormy petrel of labor-strife who had...had his bath of fire. He had no use for any temporizing labor-policy, scorned the conservative labor-leaders as a bunch of compromisers, believed in unionism* and *the strike; had passed through a Socialist phase, but found Socialism too dilatory; through a brief membership in the I.W.W., from which he had soon resigned; he was not an anarchist in any strict sense of the term; he was, in fact, difficult to classify.*

In fact, Mooney could not *be* classified. He was a loose cannon. The one thing on which everyone could agree about Mooney was that he had a genius for antagonizing people, both supporters and enemies. Businessmen thought him a dangerous radical, labor found him unwilling to work in its framework and Mooney alienated others besides. When IWW men Blackie Ford and Herman Suhr were sentenced to life imprisonment for their alleged part in the Wheatland Ranch shootout in which a district attorney and sheriff's deputy were killed, Governor Hiram Johnson refused to intervene until after the state Supreme Court had reviewed their cases. Mooney wrote to Johnson and sent copies to the newspapers:

> *The Governor's statement of his reasons for refusing to act at this time shows him up in his true colors, a cowardly cur, despicable beyond recognition, and resorting to the cunning, shrewdness, trickery and cowardice of the average district attorney…*
>
> *There are some workers at least, Governor Johnson, who will not accept as final your decision on the Ford and Suhr case, and from now on they will attempt to use the only kind of reasoning that will eventually reach you, and we hope it will be indulged in until Ford and Suhr are out of jail.*
>
> *And if violence is committed, Governor Johnson is responsible for it, as he has closed the last legal or governmental avenue of action.*

For all his militancy, Mooney was not involved in a strike until early 1913, when employees of a local shoe manufacturer named Frank & Hyman struck over lowered wages. When the firm brought in scabs, Mooney followed them on his secondhand motorcycle to their homes, where Boot and Shoe Workers' Union officials asked them to walk out on the job. The strike leader also recruited one Warren Knox Billings to pose as a scab and inform to union officials. Born on July 4, 1893, Billings was an itinerant shoe lining cutter from New York State who had come west with the vague idea of joining Pancho Villa's guerrillas in Mexico. He was to report to union officials daily, but as the regular strike meeting places were being watched, it was arranged for him to go to the house on Fifteenth Street shared by Tom and Rena Mooney; Tom's brother, John; sister Anna; and mother Mary. Billings was only nineteen and looked younger, being five-foot-four and just over 120 pounds, with a thin face, fair complexion sometimes troubled by psoriasis, sandy hair and blue eyes. He was the physical opposite of the stocky, older and taller "Black Irish" Mooney, but like Mooney, he was hard to miss or mistake. A feisty sort, he got into a fight with a company guard. His pistol went off, and the bullet went through his left thumb, mangling it, and hit the guard in the foot. Arrested for assault, Billings spent two months in jail before being acquitted in a directed verdict in the court of Judge Frank Dunne of graft prosecution days. Then he went to live with the Mooneys.

Billings and Mooney become involved in and identified with "direct action." In the summer of 1913, a radical wing of the Electrical Workers struck the Pacific Gas and Electric Company (PG&E). As picketing would be ineffective or impossible against utilities transmission, strikers used sabotage: pulling down electrical wires with ropes tied to automobiles, tossing chains over adjoining lines to cause short circuits and dynamiting power towers. The jobs were in

Warren K. Billings. This photo was taken in about 1930, but Billings, aged thirty-seven, looks young and boyish. *San Francisco Public Library History Room.*

rural areas, but PG&E hired guards and detectives. Billings was detailed to learn which towers were guarded and when and stole dynamite from construction jobs.

On Thursday, September 11, Billings would testify, he was approached at the Waldorf Bar, just downstairs at 1095 Market Street from strike headquarters, by Edgar Hurley, a union official. Hurley asked Billings if he would take a suitcase to Sacramento, for which he would be paid twenty-five dollars and carfare. That was extraordinarily good pay for less than a day's work, which must have made Billings suspicious, but he maintained that he did not ask what was in the suitcase. On Saturday the thirteenth, Billings picked up the suitcase, which he was told to handle carefully, and took the train to Sacramento. When he got off, his contact was not there. In fact, his contact was Mooney, but Mooney, coming up on his motorcycle, had been caught in a traffic jam. Billings took a streetcar to the Silver Cup Saloon and set down the suitcase. That was supposed to signal his next contact, but it actually signaled police and PG&E detectives who had been following Billings since he got off the train.

It was a setup. According to Billings's later testimony, Hurley himself was supposed to have taken the suitcase to Sacramento, but for whatever reason, Hurley passed the job along. A union traitor supplied the suitcase, in which the detectives found dynamite. One of the detectives was puzzled, as Billings did not match Hurley's description. "He isn't the man," said the detective, "but that is the suitcase." "Yes, that's the suitcase all right," said another detective. The second was Martin Swanson, a blond, blue-eyed thirty-five-year-old Swede with a discernible accent. They found on Billings percussion caps, a revolver, cartridges and burglars' tools. Billings was tried for and convicted of transporting explosives

The only known photo of Martin Swanson, undated (and possibly retouched). *Bancroft Library*.

on a public conveyance and sentenced to two years in Folsom Prison, in the Sierra foothills above Sacramento.

Apparently learning that Swanson was after him, Mooney grew a mustache and hid out in Northern California until December 1913, when he took a mysterious "fishing trip" with two electrical workers named Hanlon and Brown to San Pablo Bay, a northern arm of San Francisco Bay, in an old secondhand skiff. The skiff took on water, and after bailing it out and running it aground near Richmond, Contra Costa County, Mooney, Hanlon and Brown went ashore to sleep. When they returned, they were arrested. PG&E detectives had found the skiff full of weapons, ammunition, batteries wired to an alarm clock, blasting caps and wire.

As they were being held pending trial, *Bulletin* labor editor Ely reported that the San Francisco Labor Council protested against their inhumane treatment. Other progressives, including Cora Older, also protested. Three trials for attempted sabotage followed, with PG&E attorneys supposedly assisting the prosecution but actually conducting it. The International Workers Defense League (IWDL) hired attorneys for Mooney, the primary one being Maxwell McNutt, who, in another twist of fate, had prosecuted Billings in the assault case but had left the San Francisco district attorney's office in disgust over the way Fickert ran it—or, more accurately, did not run it. The defense charged that it was a frame-up, saying that the weapons and other paraphernalia were put in the skiff by PG&E operatives, and Mooney was acquitted in the third and final trial. PG&E attorney John Barrett told McNutt something like, "Well, Mac, you got Mooney out this time, but we put a red shirt on the son-of-a-bitch, and we will get something on him some day." Older drew a parallel with *Les Misérables*, saying that Swanson the detective followed Mooney as obsessively as Javert had followed Jean Valjean.

An assessment of Billings and Mooney must conclude that they were labor figures but not labor leaders. Billings was on labor's periphery, a worker at odd jobs who might have settled into regular employment if he had a chance to mature; he was, after all, only nineteen when he came to San Francisco.

BILLINGS WAS RELEASED from Folsom Prison on parole in December 1914 after just over a year. He had studied bookkeeping there, and Older found him a job keeping books for a tailor, after which Billings kept books for the IWDL. He also worked as an automobile mechanic, among other things.

Work in Mooney's trade was scarce. He had worked at the Underwood Typewriter exhibit at the PPIE, but in 1916, Rena's music teaching provided their only regular income. Tom and Rena lived at her studio to save rent. When Duffus met Mooney in Ely's office at the *Bulletin*, he was on yet another tack. Mooney had worked with striking shoemakers and striking electrical workers, although he was unaffiliated with either, and now, although he was not a car man, he was trying to organize the URR car men (nonunion since the bitter strike of 1907) and get them to strike again. Duffus, in the only question he would ever ask Mooney, asked if could get those fellows to come out on strike. Mooney looked at Duffus sourly and growled, "I'll pull them. Wait and see." Mooney, said Duffus, was not appealing and had no charm.

Patrick Calhoun had been forced out of the presidency of the URR, and his misuse of funds had left the company in bad shape. Crews were overworked and underpaid, service was poor and there was competition from the public Municipal Railway and from the jitneys. Still, the URR continued to spend money on informers and detectives, one of the latter being Martin Swanson, also head detective for a combine of utility companies, including the one that supplied power to the URR. On June 10, Mooney held a prestrike meeting that probably drew as many detectives and informers as it did union men. The same day, the URR posted a notice in its car barns:

> *This is to inform you that one Thomas J. Mooney, a molder by trade, but at present unemployed, who was arrested and confined in jail as a dynamiter for his activities during the Pacific Gas and Electric Company's strike in 1913, is at present endeavoring to enroll some of our employees in the Car Men's Union. It is needless to advise you that the Company is familiar with his every move and takes this occasion to notify you that any man found to be affiliated with Mooney, or any union, will be promptly discharged.*

Having been acquitted in Martinez of being a "dynamiter," Mooney tried to file a criminal complaint because of the reference, but his attorney advised him that it would be useless due to the hostility of the district attorney's office. Mooney tried unsuccessfully to get the San Francisco Labor Council to endorse his strike plans and then called a wildcat strike. It was a fiasco. At 5:30 p.m. on Friday, July 14, a streetcar going east down Geary stopped across the tracks of both the URR and the Municipal Railway. Streetcar traffic was blocked from the Ferry Building to Ninth Street, and "Strike" was shouted. The operators were exhorted to leave their places, but few did—possibly just one. Several people were arrested, including Rena Mooney, accused of trying to climb over the front wire door of a car. It was over in an hour, and the next day, San Franciscans were reading again about Tom Mooney.

Saturday, July 22, 1916

Preparedness Day

New York City had held a Preparedness parade on Saturday, May 13—150,000 New Yorkers marching down Fifth Avenue for twelve hours. An anonymous announcement reported that staging the parade would cost $500,000, "but the Captains of Industry feel that the money will not be spent in vain." The *Bulletin* called this a giveaway that Preparedness was a scheme by high finance to get fat government contracts. It noted that labor unions did not participate and said that there was no likelihood that they would in Preparedness parades in San Francisco or Chicago:

> *There is a reason. Union labor does not think that the men who are leading the preparedness campaign are coming to them with clean hands. They see as eager advocates of preparedness—yes, of militarism—the very men who are the most active foes of all labor organizations—the despots of big business, the smug tyrants of "company towns," the cold-blooded financiers whose influence is always thrown against democracy. The sight makes them draw back suspiciously. There is no magic in preparedness that will turn such enemies into friendly allies.*

San Francisco's parade was scheduled for Saturday, July 22. Units were to assemble at the Embarcadero, which runs almost at a right angle to the end of Market Street in front of the Ferry Building, and along Steuart, the next street west. At 1:30 p.m., about twenty thousand marchers would begin to go southwest up Market Street, and when the grand marshal reached

Civic Center, the units would halt while bands played the national anthem in unison. The parade would take about six hours, during which Market Street would be closed to all traffic except ambulances, should any be necessary. Access to side streets would be blocked by ropes.

In the weeks before the parade, San Francisco newspapers covered it endlessly. Hearst's *Examiner* ran picture after picture of units practicing, bands rehearsing and girls saluting. It quoted both Mullally ("We must make this a thorough, red-blooded American demonstration in every sense of the word") and Chairman of the Pacific Coast Defense League Charles Hanlon ("Every red-blooded American in San Francisco is aroused"). There was an implication that anyone not aroused or participating was unpatriotic or effeminate. The *Call* and *Chronicle* also covered parade plans, the *Chronicle* less enthusiastically as it was staunchly Republican and there was a Democratic administration in Washington.

The *Bulletin* gave minimal coverage to Preparedness and maximum coverage to its critics. An anti-Preparedness meeting would be held at the Dreamland Skating Rink on Thursday the twentieth, two days before the parade. Rudolph Spreckels was chairman. Speakers would include Spreckels, Rabbi Jacob Nieto of Sherith Israel, Secretary of the Building Trades Council Olaf Tveitmoe, San Francisco election commissioner William McDevitt, suffragist leader and poet Sara Bard Field (the Olders' neighbor) and Mrs. David Starr Jordan, wife of Stanford University's first president and a prominent suffragist and peace advocate. On the speakers' platform would be businessmen, academics, clergy, labor leaders, journalists, literati, IWDL members and a few anarchists, not violent ones. It was a broad group, many of whom had disagreed with one another vehemently on other issues, but they were all united against militarism and Hearst (it does not appear that the Olders attended).

EARLY IN THE MORNING of June 11, just after the meeting during which Mooney tried to rally the car men to strike the URR, a dynamite explosion damaged three utility towers of the company that supplied electric power to the URR, in the San Bruno Mountains south of San Francisco. The site is difficult to access, and Mooney could not have gotten there in time to place a bomb, but Swanson's operatives apparently spread rumors that he was involved, and the URR offered a reward of $5,000 for evidence leading to the conviction of the perpetrators. Four days before the Preparedness Day parade, Martin Swanson found Billings, who was between jobs, showed him the reward notice and asked about Mooney's involvement with the San

Israel Weinberg, circa 1916. *From* The Survey, *July 7, 1917.*

Bruno bombing. Billings played along, hoping to get money out of Swanson, and then went to Mooney. Mooney told him to not have anything to do with Swanson, and when Billings saw Swanson again, he accused him of trying to frame Mooney.

The same week, one Israel Weinberg, a Russian immigrant jitney driver whose son took piano lessons from Rena Mooney, was driving his machine when it was boarded by a husky man whom Weinberg had never met. The man asked Weinberg to drive him to the Seven Mile House, at the northwest corner of San Francisco, and as they went, the man said, "If Mooney would be able to pull off a car strike, you jitney drivers would be doing pretty good." The stranger added that jitney business was slow. Weinberg agreeing, the stranger snapped his fingers and said, "You could make five thousand dollars as easy as *that*!"

"That's fine," said Weinberg skeptically. "Tell me how."

"You know Mooney?"

"Yes, I know Mooney."

"You know that the towers were blown up, don't you?"

"I don't know if they were or not," Weinberg answered cautiously.

"A few days ago you received a notice from the United Railroads offering five thousand dollars for any information leading to the arrest of the fellows that blew up the towers."

Weinberg had received such a notice. "Are you a police officer?" he asked.

"No. My name is Martin Swanson. I am a detective with the United Railroads. I want you to tell me all about Mooney. And if not, I'll take the matter up with the chief [of police] and he will take away your jitney license." Weinberg denied that this could be done. Swanson retorted that it could. Weinberg said that he could make a living anyhow.

"Listen, Weinberg. It's no use for you to talk like that. It's easier for you to make five thousand dollars," Swanson continued. "It wouldn't take much to convict them—just a little circumstantial evidence—it wouldn't be necessary for you to say you remembered all the details." Referring to a picnic to which Weinberg had driven the Mooneys as payment for Weinberg's son's music lessons, Swanson said, "We can prove that he was riding in your machine and that you took him to a picnic and he was going to your house. That's enough information. It will be easy enough to convict Mooney. A fellow like you will get five thousand dollars, and you can go from here to New York and start in business."

"I hope you get the man you want," said Weinberg, "but please leave me alone."

Two days later, Swanson boarded Weinberg's jitney again. "Listen. I was talking with Mr. Abbott [URR attorney, indicted during the graft prosecution], and if you don't know enough to secure a conviction, we will pay you for what you do know, and keep your name strictly confidential."

"No please, Mr. Swanson, I have told you I have got troubles enough of my own. And really, I don't know what to tell you."

"Do you want to go and see Mr. Abbott, or don't you?" asked Swanson.

"I have nothing to see anybody about."

"Is that the way you feel about it?"

"Yes."

Swanson shoved a nickel at Weinberg, got out, slammed the jitney door and said, "I'll get you yet."

The anti-Preparedness meeting on Thursday the twentieth was packed. A band played. Rudolph Spreckels got a standing ovation, and his speech showed the same dedication to principle that he had shown during the graft prosecution:

> *I am not here to represent the capitalistic class. I haven't been asked to speak for them. I am here to raise my voice with those who believe that humanity has rights that are paramount to all others. If I had one dirty dollar I wouldn't be here. I think that you will realize that with the capitalistic class of this community against me—some of them having been prosecuted through my own efforts—and with the subsidized press hating me bitterly, that there is nothing discreditable in my career that you wouldn't know if they could possibly tell it to you.*
>
> *I come here tonight with a kindly feeling and good will towards all those who live on this earth with you and me. I am surprised by the utter lack of appreciation of their own position displayed by those men who prate of patriotism and Preparedness. They are utterly lacking in that sense of humor that is sometimes a saving grace.*

Who is it that has organized this parade and will march in it on Saturday? Why, the public service corporations who have grafted upon and debauched our community, and who now stand sponsor for and claim to represent patriotism. They ought to apologize for making such a claim. There are men who will wave the flag on our streets on Saturday who should hide themselves in shame.

These men are inconsistent. They'll march on Saturday, but I haven't heard that any of them have enlisted.

I have a son who will soon be at the age when he will be eligible to enlist, but I hope to God he will never lift his hand against his fellow man unless it is to strike a blow for human liberty.

Hearst's name was hissed. Sara Bard Field called Preparedness "capitalizing fear." Rabbi Nieto commented:

Next Saturday out will walk the great, fat-bellied banker, in august panoplied grandeur, holding his hand on his stomach, or some other part of his anatomy, to make sure that he's safe. Behind him will march a man in a stove pipe hat, perhaps left over from the Exposition.

They'll pretend that they are fighting for the spirit of '76. They're not. They're fighting to hold what they've got and perhaps to get more.

What's really going to happen on Saturday? Oh, that I had the combined gifts of Gilbert and Sullivan, that I might construct a comic opera to fit the occasion!

The speech that would get the most notoriety—not immediately, but later—was by McDevitt, who also ran a bookstore specializing in radical literature. McDevitt spoke generally of the brotherhood of man and against war, but somewhere he paraphrased George Bernard Shaw, who in an interview by Mary Boyle O'Reilly of the *New York Call* had heaped sarcasm on all the belligerent nations. "The Junker caste of Germany is no better, no worse, than the junker [*sic*] caste of England," said Shaw. "Commanding troops is the only aristocratic profession. The German people hate the military caste as do the English people—and for the same reasons. In both armies THE SOLDERS SHOULD SHOOT THEIR OFFICERS AND GO HOME, the agriculturalist to his land and the townsman to his painting and glazing."

"That was the advice of Bernard Shaw," said McDevitt. "If I thought the people in the Preparedness parade on Saturday afternoon were in a heroic humor and could take sound advice, I might be tempted to say to them 'Shoot in the back of the neck, or somewhere else, in this parade, all of the corrupt corporation officials and minions, all of the corrupt bankers, all of the representatives of those powers whose greed is lust for war, shoot them and call it a good day's work and come home.'"

The *Chronicle* printed a short account of the rally. The *Examiner* ran a shorter one under the headline, "Anti-Preparedness Talk Pleases Few": "Three thousand persons attended the beginning of last night's meeting at Dreamland to hear addresses against making preparations for the defense of the nation. The audience decreased in size as the meeting progressed."

The *Bulletin* called that "a purported news account of last night's enthusiastic mass meeting for peace. It is a fine specimen of the Hearst poison method of misleading his readers."

On Friday the twenty-first, organized labor passed two resolutions. One, by the Building Trades Council—referring to threats by "certain employers, superintendents, and their agents" that union workers would lose their jobs if they did not march in Saturday's parade—advised union men to "resent the threats hereinbefore referred to as a flagrant invasion of their personal and legal rights" and advised that the council would assist them if they did lose their jobs. The other, by the San Francisco Labor Council, referred to rumors that labor's enemies were concocting some kind of "disturbance":

> *Whereas, it has come to our attention that, because united labor is opposed to the fostering of the war spirit by "preparedness parades," an attempt may be made by the enemies of labor to cause a violent disturbance during the… parade and charge that disturbance to labor in the hope of discrediting labor organizations in the eyes of our citizens generally:*
>
> *Therefore, be it resolved: That in order to forestall any possible frame-up of this character…we hereby caution all union men and women… to be especially careful and make no other protest that their silent non-participation on the preparedness parade.*

There were other rumors and threats. For weeks before Saturday the twenty-second, someone had been sending anonymous postcards to chamber of commerce members and others connected with the parade. One read:

> *Your extreme activity in promoting and glorifying militarism, marks you as the most vicious and dangerous "jingo" of all your brutal, greedy, thieving, and war-making class; and the immediate "extermination" of you and your evil class, is going to be the sole and "patriotic" duty of the*
>
> *Employees Liberty League*

Older also got a threat, although for once it was not against him personally. On Friday the twenty-first, a crudely hand-printed letter arrived at the *Bulletin*:

> *The Editor of the Bulletin*
>
> *Our protests have been in vain in regards to this preparedness prorroganda* [sic], *so we are going to use a little direct action on the 22nd which will echo around the earth and show that frisco really knows how, and that militarism cant be forced on us and our children without a violent protest. Things are going to happen to show that we will go to any extreme, the same as the controlling class, to preserve what little democracy we still have, dont take this as a joke or you will be rudely awaken, we have sworn to do our duty to the masses and only send this warning to those who are wise but forced to march to hold their jobs, as we want to give only the hypocritical patriots who shout for war but never go a real taste of war. Kindly ask the chamber of commerce to march in a solid body, if they want to prove they are not cowards. Our duty has been done so far, thank Mr. Older for his great work of the past in enlightening the masses and hope he will never allow himself to become the intellectual prostitute as the other dailys. A copy has been sent to all dailys.*
>
> *The determined exiles from militaristic governments*
>
> *U.S.* *Russia*
> *Holland* *Germany*
> *Italy*

Older sent the letter to Chief of Police White. The identities of the writers of the postcards and the letter were never learned.

San Francisco summers are notoriously foggy and cold, but Saturday was warm, sunny and sultry. It was uncomfortable for marching but a good day to watch. The morning editions of the *Chronicle* and *Examiner* ran the expected coverage. A front-page *Chronicle* headline read, "Patriots' Pageant to Cry Prepare." The front page also had a two-column cut of a bird's-eye drawing of Market Street seen from above the Ferry Building. In the lower-left corner was "Ex-Members of National Guard Meet at Steuart Street 1:15." The *Examiner* ran a picture of veterans of the First California regiment of the Spanish-American War displaying their bullet-riddled flag and noted that veterans would assemble

Bird's-eye diagram from above the Ferry Building of the parade. Note the reference to Steuart Street, *left*. *From the* Chronicle, *July 22, 1916.*

on Steuart to march up Market behind the flag remnants. Both papers, in short, mentioned Steuart Street prominently.

At the Eilers Building, Tom Mooney wrote a report on the abortive car men's strike as Rena went out to have breakfast and run some errands. He went to breakfast himself and returned after his own errands as flags were being hung along Market Street, including one on the Eilers Building. The building's music store, like most other Market Street businesses, would close for the parade, and several employees went to the roof, where they had a good view. The Mooneys, although they had no use for the parade sentiments, went to the roof themselves at about 1:30 p.m., when they heard bands playing on Market. They were joined by Rena's sister, Belle, and would stay on the roof until after 3:00 p.m. Wade Hamilton, another Eilers employee and an amateur photographer, took pictures from the roof of an adjoining building, some of which showed the Mooneys and others on the Eilers roof watching the parade below.

Billings was out and about but very differently engaged. The Machinists' Union had struck several automobile agencies, and Billings, in a repeat of his tactics during the shoemakers' strike, had posed as a scab until he was found out and fired. On Saturday morning, he was sabotaging new automobiles from a list given to him by the union. In the retail store area, around the alley known then as Union Square Avenue and today as Maiden Lane, Billings was spraying paint-remover on the cars' sides with a bulb syringe, the object being to have the cars taken in by the new owners for repainting under warranty by the agencies. The expense would be such a nuisance that the agencies would negotiate with the union without necessarily acknowledging why. One vehicle was a Hudson owned by Dr. Robert Patek, who was taking Judge Dunne to the ferry. Billings was relieved when they drove off without noticing the stripe on the car or Billings himself.

Saturday was a *Bulletin* workday. Duffus and his young wife were living in Palo Alto, and he commuted on the same peninsula route to San Francisco as Older from Cupertino. Duffus had come to drop off some editorials, write another, take them to the composing room and take the train back. Older, city editor Carl Hoffman, sports editor Edgar ("Scoop") Gleeson and Ernest Hopkins were all working. Also in San Francisco was Stewart ("Stu") Dunbar, a veteran reporter who had filled in for vacationing reporters but had been laid off. Dunbar had installed a new engine in an old fishing boat and had gone to a marine supply store on Steuart Street to purchase paint and probably other materials, planning to take a little voyage before facing the reality of being out of a job.

At about 12:45 p.m., forty-five minutes before the parade was scheduled to begin, tobacconist John Clifton saw two men by his business at Kearny and California Streets, north of Market about three-quarters of a mile west of the Ferry Building. Both were dark-complexioned, suggesting they were Greek, Italian or Mexican. One was about thirty-five, about five feet, ten inches and 160 pounds. The other was about thirty, about five feet, six inches and somewhat heavyset, about 140 pounds. They were poorly dressed—the older man in an old, rough blue suit and worn soft black hat and the younger in a dark-gray suit and dark-green hat. They had a suitcase, a cheap worn one, brown or tan and apparently heavy. Clifton saw them board the California Street cable car, and conductor Samuel Weeks saw them get off at Market. Weeks thought it strange for two obviously poor men to ride the car for such a short distance, and like Clifton, he noted their appearance. His description matched that by Clifton almost exactly.

At about 1:40 p.m., by his account, John Powers, a working man who lived at Eleventh and Folsom, was going south down Steuart Street when he saw a man come north up the block and set a tan, cheap suitcase by the wall of the Ferry Exchange Saloon, on the west side just south of Market. Powers described the man as "apparently a Mexican," about five feet, four inches and 130 pounds, wearing a dark suit and broad-brimmed hat, possibly a sombrero. As veterans of the Grand Army of the Republic (GAR) were assembling on Steuart, Major W.J. Watson saw the suitcase, although he had the time at about 1:25 p.m. Noticing that nobody seemed to own it, he said he "was about to go up and give it a kick to see what it contained, but on second thought decided not to…It was of imitation leather, terra cotta color…well worn and broken a little at the corners." Elmer E. Kimberlin, who had been a night watchman at the PPIE, was standing by the saloon about 1:30 p.m. when he saw a man coming up Steuart, as Powers had, carrying a suitcase that he set down by the saloon. Kimberlin's description varied from that by Powers, Kimberlin's man being about five feet, ten inches and about 170 pounds, but his description matched that of the larger man seen by Clifton and Weeks, including the suit, the black hat and the dark complexion. Kimberlin crossed Steuart Street and saw several people go up to the suitcase, including thirteen-year-old Jimmy McDougall, who sat on it for a while.

Three more witnesses saw one or both men. Charles Johnson, a ship's carpenter and San Mateo County deputy sheriff, said that a dark-complexioned man, about five-foot-seven and about 160 pounds, with black hair, wearing a dark crush (soft) hat, put a suitcase by the saloon wall and walked off. Johnson caught up with the man and asked him why he had left the suitcase there. The man said he did not want it and walked ahead very fast without looking at Johnson, but Johnson said that he saw the man board a boat for Seattle the next Monday. The man saw Johnson looking at him and walked away. Ex-seaman William H. Taylor had been in the saloon, and coming out he saw a man about five feet, seven or eight inches, with kind of a sallow complexion, put the suitcase against the building wall. Taylor said, "That is a bad place to put it, my friend, for this crowd is around here and somebody will come along and pick it up." Taylor said the man turned around and said, "Don't you touch that suitcase, I know what I am doing." M.T. Pendergast, a gardener and Spanish-American War veteran, also said that he saw a man whom he described as Mexican or Portuguese, about twenty-five, five-foot-eight and about 145 pounds, put the suitcase on the sidewalk. He was sure that there was another man with him, but that may have been Taylor.

One last witness was John McDonald, an itinerant waiter recently discharged from the hospital after stomach surgery. McDonald said that as he stood at the northeast corner of Steuart and Market, he saw a "dirty-looking" man with a dark complexion, thirty to thirty-five years old, five feet, seven or eight inches, about 150 pounds, come north up the west side of Steuart Street, the route taken by Powers's and Kimberlin's man, and set a tan suitcase by the saloon wall. Another man came out of the saloon, said McDonald, this one twenty-five to thirty years old, about five-foot-eight and 145 pounds, with a medium complexion and wearing a blue suit and gray hat. They talked, and then the man who had set down the suitcase continued in the direction in which he had come and crossed Market Street in a northerly direction. The other stayed a few minutes longer, with an occasional glance at the suitcase, and then also went up to Market and crossed in a westerly direction. McDonald's testimony was suspect. He would have been on the opposite side of the street from the saloon, about sixty feet away, the street was crowded and McDonald was short and could not have seen over the assembling marchers even if he were on the curb.

At 1:30 p.m., Police Lieutenant Duncan Matheson blew his whistle at Steuart and Market Streets. Thornwell Mullally led off on a bay horse, followed a minute later by, of course, Sunny Jim Rolph. At the *Bulletin*, almost one mile up Market, Hopkins and Gleeson perched on the fire escape outside the editorial rooms, Hopkins taking notes as Gleeson pointed out details. Both remarked on something that they could sense but not use. The atmosphere of the crowd, banked eight to ten deep on the sidewalks four stories below, "was queerly tense…this was like no other public event we had seen. Something was in the air." Duffus would work another hour before taking the train home and wouldn't lose time on the parade, but he thought he'd have a look from Carl Hoffman's window. Older was in his office with his back to the window. The war fury made him sick.

By 1:58 p.m., the parade had passed the *Bulletin* and stopped at Fifth Street to rest and catch up. Back at Steuart, the GAR unit was poised to move out when seventy-two-year-old Adam Fox, who had enlisted in 1862, collapsed from the heat. An ambulance was called, and his fellow veterans carried him into a store on the east side of the block to wait. "You can get along all right, boys," Fox told them.

At 2:06 p.m., the ambulance attendants were lifting Fox onto a stretcher when it happened: a white flash, a deafening explosion and a concussion. Metal shards, nails and bullets mowed down the crowd like a machine gun. Six people were dead or dying: George Lawlor, a lumber salesman, the top of his head blown off; Lea Lamborn, his body flung over Lawlor's; George Painter, MD, a friend of Rolph's who would die that night with Rolph at his bedside; Mrs. Hetta Knapp, who was standing next to her husband and son; Arthur Nelson, a commissary clerk at the Fairmont Hotel; and Fox, who would die from shock. Four others would die later. Mangled victims lay on the street, and screams and moans came from the dying and the wounded, as well as their friends and relatives. Blood and blown-out window glass were everywhere, there were holes in the bricks and sidewalk where the suitcase had been and a pall of white smoke was rising over the block.

Stu Dunbar was walking out of the marine supply store when the bomb exploded and was knocked back but unhurt. He saw the prone bodies—some motionless, others writhing in pain—saw chunks of flesh, smelled the stench of smoke and, assuming that he was rehired, got to a telephone. On the *Bulletin* fire escape, Hopkins and Gleeson sensed a vague, distant commotion, coming from somewhere down Market Street. Hopkins had a sensation of something snapping, like the string of a violin in its case. They craned over the railing but saw nothing different, just the crowds as before and perhaps a faint white cloud. Gleeson said, "I'm going down there," crawled back through the window and ran for the elevator. Carl Hoffman came out, "You know, there were warning letters sent through the mails. We got one yesterday; handed it over to the police. Get ready, if it's a story. I'll take the phones." Hopkins hauled his lanky form back in. Duffus was still in

Steuart Street after the bomb. Dead bodies covered by sheets may be those of George Lawlor and Lea Lanborn. *Author's collection.*

Hoffman's office when all the phones in the city room rang at once, and his heart skipped a beat. Hoffman grabbed a phone, and Hopkins and Duffus saw the expression on his face. "Bomb explosion!" he said.

Matheson, unhurt, was faced with evacuating the dying and wounded and keeping the parade going. The ambulance that had been called for Fox took other victims to the hospital, and trucks and other vehicles were commandeered. Matheson had to meet a contingent of marchers from Oakland and put Lieutenant Stephen Bunner and some plainclothes detectives in charge of the carnage and left, not to return for more than an hour.

By the Palace Hotel, about half a mile above Steuart Street, nine-year-old newsboy George Davis heard the concussion. Thinking that a gas main had exploded, he ran with his newspapers down Market Street as a crowd gathered at Steuart. Davis and the crowd watched the attendants lifting the dying and wounded onto stretchers. As the last were carried away, Davis saw Officer Bunner commandeer a fire hose and begin washing down the sidewalk and street: blood, shreds of clothing, broken glass, wood splinters, bomb parts and even body parts went down the sewer. When Lieutenant Matheson returned to Steuart Street, he saw Bunner with the hose and said, "Bunner, what in hell are you doing?"

"I'm cleaning up," was the response.

Police hose down Steuart Street after the bomb explosion as a crowd watches. The boy carrying something under his arm may be nine-year-old George Davis. *Bancroft Library.*

About fifteen minutes later, Davis saw men in suits, whom the officers knew, arrive. There was a conversation, and then an officer fetched a sledgehammer. One of the men began pounding around the holes in the sidewalk and the saloon wall, enlarging them. Two of the men were Frederick Colburn of the chamber of commerce and District Attorney Charles Fickert. The evidentiary value of the bomb scene was completely compromised by the police and the district attorney.

Looking out Hoffman's window, Duffus saw an open truck coming west up Market carrying limp, bloodied figures. He couldn't tell if they were dead or alive until a man rose from the bed and shook his fist wildly at the building. Hopkins remembered the rest of the afternoon as a blur. Dunbar had gone to Harbor Emergency Hospital after calling Hoffman and did double duty helping the attendants and phoning in details on dead and wounded. Gleeson elbowed his way through the Market Street crowds and reached Steuart in fifteen minutes and then called for a cameraman. As the sickening details poured in, it became obvious that this was one of

BARGAINS of all kinds are found through the Classified Advertising Columns of THE CHRONICLE

San Francisco Chronicle

LEADING NEWSPAPER of the PACIFIC COAST

FOUNDED 1865 — SAN FRANCISCO, CAL., SUNDAY, JULY 23, 1916 — VOL. CIX, NO. 8

BOMB EXPLOSION KILLS 6 AND MAIMS 40 PREPAREDNESS PARADE SPECTATORS

TIMED INFERNAL MACHINE WORKS HAVOC IN CROWD

Pipe, Filled With Dynamite, Surrounded by Slugs of Jagged Metal and Bullets, More Deadly Than Shrapnel Used in Grim Work of War, Strikes Down Innocent and Peaceful Citizens, Among Them Mothers With Babes in Arms

Rolph Orders Sweeping Investigation; Police Drop All Else to Hunt Down Human Monster; Finnish Sailor Arrested as Suspect; Grand Army Veterans, Schooled Amid Shot and Shell, Prevent Panic of Paraders by Coolness

WHILE veteran soldiers of the Grand Army of the Republic, symbolizing liberty and the preservation of the Union and government, swung into the line of the preparedness parade at Steuart and Market streets, shortly after 2 o'clock yesterday, a bomb exploded six lives were snuffed out and two scores of persons, all spectators, were injured. Two of these are dying.

The police theory of the explosion is that it was the act of an anarchist or fanatic. Threatening letters had been received by proponents of the parade, the police and the newspapers for a week preceding yesterday.

No one had taken these warnings seriously. The bomb which exploded, it is thought by the police, was placed on the sidewalk, next to the brick wall of the Ferry Exchange saloon, with a time fuse or clock attachment.

As near as can be ascertained, the explosive in the deadly machine of destruction was dynamite incased in a lead pipe, surrounded by missiles. The fanatic who prepared the bomb filled it with steel rivets, cartridges, sections of steel auto tire and bul-

LIST OF DEAD, DYING AND INJURED

THE DEAD

FOX, ADAM, 3227 Sacramento street; G. A. R. veteran, 72 years of age; died from shock of explosion.
KNAPP, MRS. H. E., 1438 Sixth street, Alameda; badly mangled.
LAMBORN, L. H., 1516 St. Charles street, Alameda.
LAWLOR, GEORGE G., lumber salesman, Mill Valley.
NELSON, ARTHUR, commissary clerk, Fairmont Hotel; residence, Larkspur, Marin county.
PAINTER, DR. GEORGE L., physician, 3016 Telegraph avenue, Berkeley; lungs punctured through both sides; ribs fractured; died at Central Emergency at 6 P. M.

THE DYING

At Central Emergency Hospital.
SEEMANN, MISS PEARL, 619 Forty-fifth street, Oakland; left leg blown off.
TURNBULL, THOMAS H., 1680 California street; fractured skull.

THE INJURED

ANDERSON, A. B., printer, San Anselmo, lacerations of both legs and of the body.
ANDERSON, THOMAS, 50 Clay street, powder burns in the face and cuts.
BRYDON, C. A., 1612 Minton avenue; Alameda, contusions and abrasion of face.
BRYDON, MRS. C. A., 1612 Minton avenue, Alameda; contusions and abrasion of right leg.
BRADY, JOHN, San Bruno, severe lacerations of both legs.
CLAUSSEN, HENRY J., 725 Santa Clara avenue, Alameda, right leg fractured and severe contusions of both legs.
DETRICK HENRY L., stationer, 1815 Third avenue, Los Angeles, brother of Charles R. Detrick, secretary State Railroad Commission, severe lacerations of scalp.
GADDY, FRANCIS D., traffic officer, 327 Twenty-fifth avenue, slightly injured.
GAMMEL, RAY, traveling salesman, 556 Jones street, lacerations of legs.
KENNEDY, CAPTAIN THOMAS, 619 Forty-fifth street, Oakland; contusions of body.
KENNEDY, GEORGE, 6, son of Captain Thomas A. Kennedy, 619 Forty-fifth street, Oakland; legs cut to bone.
KENNEDY, MRS. ELEANOR, his mother; cut.
KNAPP, HOWARD E., 1436 Sixth street, Alameda, side and shoulder torn. (Mrs. Knapp was killed.)
KNAPP, WILLIAM, two and one-half years old son of Howard E. Knapp, forehead bruised and legs cut.
LOZOVSKY, GIRSH, clerk, 1380 Golden Gate avenue; right leg broken, both legs lacerated.
MEYERS, HYMAN, 1281 Vallejo street, advertising man, contusions of legs.
McARTHUR, JAMES, 32, driller, 3361 Sixteenth street; lacerations and abrasion of left leg.
McCARTHY, JERRY, Oakland, right leg cut.
McDERMOTT, JAMES, 2532 Army street; on opposite side of street; cut by glass.
MRS. McDERMOTT, his wife; shock.
MOFFET, SAMUEL, Harbor Hotel, San Francisco; laceration of hip, fractured finger.
MONROE, GEORGE D., 4096 Seventeenth street; lacerated wound of right fore arm.
NELSON, H. K., 1004 Fifty-Ninth street, Oakland; puncture wound, back.
NORN, EMIL, mechanic, American Hotel, 718 Howard street, laceration of legs.
PELSINGER, FRANCIS, 192 Sixth street, employe of Emporium.
POWELL, A. B., stevedore, 132 East street, left leg broken.
TOY SING, 15, Chinese, 658 Jackson street; laceration of back.
TCHI ONG, 14-year-old Chinese boy, 873 Washington street; cuts.
TERRY, T. J., Nevada State Superintendent of Schools, East Ely, Nev.; shock and superficial neck wounds.
TERRY, MRS. T. J., shock and neck wounds.
TOWNSEND, MISS MYRA; cuts, right leg.
VAN LOO, MRS. KINGSLEY, 384 Clark street, Oakland, gashes on leg, cuts on breast.
VAN LOO, MARIE, aged 7, cuts on left leg.
VAN LOO, RICHARD, aged 9, right foot mangled.
VAUGHAN, REUBEN J., captain of river steamer Sacramento, 2917 Lorina street, Berkeley, right leg badly mangled.
WYMORE, MRS. CECIL, 1238 Fifty-third avenue, Oakland, one leg almost blown off, and the knee on the other punctured.
WYWOOD, ROBERT, 370 First street, lacerations and bruises.
WOO YUNG, 924 Dupont street; contusions left thigh.

51,000 MARCHERS CARRY FLAGS IN IMPOSING PARADE

Well-Known San Franciscans Take Places Among Thousands of Their Fellow Citizens, Who March Quietly in One of the Most Notable Street Pageants in History of City—Seriousness of All Who Take Part Is Striking

American Emblem Displayed by Tens of Thousands and Heads of All Are Bared as National Anthem Is Played by More Than Fifty Bands—Cumulative Force of Great Display by Men and Women Proves Tremendous In Effect

Facts About the Parade

Number in line	51,329
Time occupied in passing	3 hours
Length of march	1 1-2 miles
Organizations in line	213
Bands	52

IN UNBROKEN ranks San Francisco told its determination yesterday that the United States be prepared.

It was not a holiday sentiment that the 51,000 marchers expressed, when for three hours they filed through the length of Market street, in ranks that reached from curb to curb. For in the long list of street pageants that San Francisco has known, the Preparedness of July 22 stands alone in the seriousness of its purpose and the magnitude of its declaration.

From the San Francisco Chronicle, *July 23, 1916.*

the worst crimes in San Francisco history, possibly *the* worst. The *Bulletin*'s first extra was on the streets at 2:45 p.m. and was snapped up immediately. The fourth re-plate, around 4:30 p.m., reported six dead and between forty and fifty wounded, which was accurate but had one critical error: "Some person unknown threw an explosive bomb into a dense crowd of onlookers, at Steuart and Market streets....The bomb was in a suitcase, fragments of which were blown in all direction."

A time bomb or fuse bomb—the Steuart Street one was probably an acid-fuse bomb—is not thrown, as that would risk stopping the clock or disrupting the fuse. The thrown-bomb story would become part theory, part folklore, with serious consequences.

Older said, "They'll probably blame me for this." Late that afternoon, depressed, he boarded the commute train with Hoffman and Duffus, and as they rode, he leaned forward and whispered, "I think Mooney did it." Asked why, Older said, "Process of elimination. I know most of the reds in the city, but out of all I know, Mooney is the only one rash enough to do something like this."

Older's prediction that he would get blamed came true immediately. On Monday the twenty-fourth, Hearst's *Examiner* and *Call* ran the same editorial, alleging that San Francisco was in the grip of a "Mafia" of pacifists, anarchists and coddlers of criminals:

> *So soon as some notorious anarchist comes to preach his or her doctrine of murder and arson, THERE you will find our own political and journalistic demagogues gathered together...THERE you will find our own sweet sympathizers with crime and murder, flocking to raise money for defense funds, printing maudlin and lying editorials and news apologies...and evincing in every possible form their sympathy with, if not their actual guilty foreknowledge of and connivance in the crime itself.*
>
> *...Let the punishment of these men and women who misuse their opportunities, their intellectual gifts and, sometimes, their standing and their wealth, and who abuse the noble rights of free speech and free printing, be a complete ostracism from the society of decent folks.*
>
> *...You all know who these disturbers of the community's peace and enemies of the community's welfare are.*

The "journalistic demagogue" with his "maudlin editorials and news apologies," everyone knew, was Older. The charge that he sympathized with

Note the figure "Don't Parade," a shot at Older. *From the* San Francisco Examiner, July 25, 1916.

crime or had "guilty foreknowledge and connivance in the crime itself" was viciously untrue, and on Tuesday the twenty-fifth, the *Bulletin* shot back:

> *Posing as the champion of "law, order, of loyalty and of decency," William Randolph Hearst calls upon the "Citizens" of San Francisco to "rid our city of the mean and loathsome vermin" who were responsible for the sextuple murder of Saturday...* [He] *refers vaguely to social reformers of various schools: "demagogues," "knaves," "sweet sympathizers with crime and murder," "weak-kneed officials," "preachers of class hatred." And says, "We could name in the space of one short paragraph every one of the leaders of this Mafia of graft, terrorism, disorder and crime."*
>
> *...Why doesn't Hearst name the "vermin?" Why does he stop short? Why does he froth at the mouth in an agony of words—and leave out the crux of it all?*

Preparedness forces besides Hearst took advantage of the opportunity to blame the bomb on anti-Preparedness men and women, particularly those at the Thursday night meeting. Sunday morning's *Examiner* reported, "Mullally Puts Blame for Bomb Upon Speeches" and quoted Mullally: "I attribute the crime to the incendiary work done by one of our most prominent citizens at the mass meeting held Thursday night to protest against the Preparedness parade. Because of that meeting and anonymous threats I feared something like this would happen." The *Examiner* also printed a speech at the Commercial Club by businessman Albert Castle, who said, "The crime committed on Saturday last is directly traceable to the anti-Preparedness meeting of the previous Thursday." Castle followed that teaser with non sequiturs, quoting Spreckels, McDevitt and Rabbi Nieto: "The next speech, I am ashamed to say, was made by a minister of my own faith, Dr. Nieto." Neither Mullally nor Castle produced a single fact to support the charge that anti-Preparedness had any responsibility for the bomb, let alone that the bomb was "directly traceable" to Thursday's meeting.

Duffus found it illogical that anti-Preparedness people (and the *Bulletin*), who were opposed to blowing men to bits in war, should be blamed for the Preparedness Day bombing. The *Bulletin* editorial for Monday the twenty-fourth noted, "Those who love peace and sanity do not love bombs," and added that militarists, not pacifists, were seizing on the tragedy. Duffus had put his finger on one of the biggest challenges facing pacifists and social critics, the popular belief that dissent equals disloyalty, especially in a time of physical danger.

The week after the bombing, San Francisco was the jumpiest it had been since the earthquake and fire of April 1906. Hopkins told of a news photographer who set off his flash gun in the local room, making an editor jump out of his chair and topple backward. Hopkins himself went on an overnight visit and packed a suitcase with pajamas. People edged away on the streetcars, laughed nervously and looked at him suspiciously. When he took the suitcase into an elevator, it emptied and someone shrieked, "For God's sake get that thing out of here!" Newspaper columns alternated between coverage of blaming the bomb on anti-Preparedness, Saturday's sightings of bomb suspects and deaths and funerals of victims. Mrs. Kingsley Van Loo of Oakland was standing between her two children when she was struck in the head and died on Wednesday the twenty-sixth. A looter had stripped off her jewelry as she lay on the pavement with a fractured skull.

On Sunday the twenty-third, Chief White created a bomb squad, the first in San Francisco's history. Duncan Matheson, promoted to captain, was head, assisted by detective Sergeant Charles Goff, Lieutenant Bunner and others, including rookie Draper Hand. Matheson, said Hopkins, was "undoubtedly the best policeman in the city," and Goff had been a bodyguard of Heney's during the graft prosecution, but both were basically traffic cops with no bomb experience, nor had their co-workers any. The squad was kept busy sifting through a mountain of information from witnesses who saw or claimed to have seen the men who placed the bomb, sharing information from police departments in the Bay Area and elsewhere and examining evidence. A reward fund for information leading to the arrests and conviction of the perpetrators grew fast. The city contributed $5,000, the Law and Order Committee another $5,000, the slain Lea Lanborn's brother $1,000, the state another $1,000 and anonymous and other individual donors other amounts, and by the end of the week, the total, well publicized, was more than $17,000. Meanwhile, on the evening of Saturday the twenty-second Fickert had had a visitor: Martin Swanson.

Arrests

Newspaper reports about the bomb investigation from the week of July 23 were confusing. The *Bulletin* and the *Examiner* printed stories about Clifton and Weeks seeing the two men with the suitcase on California Street, and the *Chronicle* printed the account by Powers of seeing the man with the suitcase on Steuart Street. A subhead above the *Examiner* story proclaimed, "Chief of Police Declares that Short Time Will Bring About Arrest of Men Responsible for Outrage of Last Saturday," suggesting that the men on the street were suspects. Monday's *Chronicle* reported a bomb plot: "District Attorney Fickert intimated that he has a suspicion as to the identity of the ringleaders, but, further than that, would make no statement," suggesting that other suspects, unspecified, were sought. Another article quoted Fickert charging that San Francisco was "infested with a number of wild-eyed, rabid propagandists [who] have selected San Francisco for the time being, to give expression to their hatred of government and their defiance of all institutions." A newspaper reader might conclude that any of three groups of suspects—the men on the street, a ring or some group of violent anarchists—was being taken seriously and would soon be arrested.

The bomb squad was compiling a suspect list. Prominent anarchists Emma Goldman and Alexander Berkman were in San Francisco, Goldman making speeches and Berkman publishing a newsletter unfortunately titled the *Blast*. They and other anarchists were on the list, as were Billings, Mooney and other leftists. By the morning of Wednesday the twenty-sixth, however, no arrests had been made, and the bomb squad's investigation appeared to be stalled. In fact, although Matheson and his colleagues didn't know it, their bomb squad had become subservient, and the investigation had become a vendetta. On the night of Saturday the twenty-second, Martin Swanson had been converted from a private investigator to a quasi-public one—at whose instigation was unclear—and was in de facto control of the district attorney's office concerning the bombing. The chain of command went from Swanson to Fickert to Chief White to Matheson.

On Wednesday the twenty-sixth, the *Bulletin* reported that White, Bunner and Goff had arrested a man, "name unknown," who had applied for treatment at the Lane Hospital free clinic "suffering from injuries which apparently were caused by an explosion." The unnamed man was Billings, who had been seen in the clinic regularly for treatment by a Dr. Alderman for a facial rash. Contrary to the story, Billings's rash was unrelated to any explosion, but newspapers were dependent for information on Fickert or the police, one of which had probably suggested the connection. Billings had been seen in clinic on Monday and had a follow-up appointment on Wednesday. In the waiting room, he saw Swanson, Fickert, White, Goff and Bunner coming down the corridor. Unfortunately, Billings thought that they were coming to question him about the cars he had vandalized on Saturday. Having written the license numbers of the cars on a cigarette paper in lieu of notepaper, he rolled a cigarette in the paper and lit it. That may have cost him. Swanson said, "Hi, kid." Bunner and Goff slapped the handcuffs

ROOMS are best rented through the Classified Advertising Columns of THE CHRONICLE

San Francisco Chronicle

LEADING NEWSPAPER OF THE PACIFIC COAST

FAIR — CITY Weather Report — T. S. REED, Forecaster.

FOUNDED 1865 — SAN FRANCISCO, CAL., THURSDAY, JULY 27, 1916 — VOL. CIX, NO. 12

Police Arrest Man and Woman for Bomb Murders

WARREN K. BILLINGS AND BELLE LAVIN IN PRISON AS SUSPECTS

Chief of Special Detective Bureau Declares Department Is Unearthing "Most Widespread and Terrible Conspiracy for Ruthless Destruction of Lives and Property San Francisco Has Ever Known—Two More Victims of Saturday's Crime Are Dead

Thomas J. Mooney, Agitator and Suspected Dynamiter, Disappears With His Wife From the City; 200 Steel Nosed 22-Caliber Bullets Identical With Bomb Missles Found in Billings' Room Together With a Loaded 32-Caliber Automatic Revolver

"THIS is the most widespread and terrible conspiracy for the ruthless destruction of lives and property that San Francisco has ever known."

This was the declaration of Captain of Police Duncan Matheson last night at the close of a day of high pressure action in the police effort to run to earth the perpetrators of the bomb outrage at Steuart and Market

TWO BOMB SUSPECTS SEIZED BY POLICE

Warren K. Billings, arrested at Lane Hospital, and Mrs. Belle Lavin, his landlady, taken into custody at 2410 Mission street, where the police say they found incriminating evidence. Below is a bomb container which was left by two men at a Beale-street welding works.

'PURIFY CITY' IS DEMAND AT CITIZENS' BIG MEETING

Auditorium Is Crowded With Those Who Demand an End to the Spirit of Lawlessness

RINGING RESOLUTIONS VOICE PUBLIC HORROR

Determination to Stamp Out Foes of Law and Order Is Forcibly Expressed by San Franciscans

Progress in Bomb Inquiry Digested

THE chief developments in the bomb case yesterday were:

Blacklisting

THIRD LINE IS PIERCED BY BRITISH AT POZIERES

Key to Strongly-Fortified German Positions Is Captured by Tremendous Attacks of Anzac Men

ALL ENGLAND REJOICES AT SUCCESS OF ARMY

Teuton Counter Attacks Constantly Expected on Village Cleared After Three Days and Nights of Fighting

By Arthur S. Draper

Billings and his landlady are arrested. *From the* San Francisco Chronicle, *July 27, 1916.*

on him, and as Billings was frisked, he was told that he was under arrest. "What for?" No one answered. As they went down the corridor, Bunner asked Billings who had just identified him. Billings asked, "Don't you know him?" Bunner said he didn't. Billings said it was Swanson, a URR detective.

On Thursday, the morning newspapers reported Billings's arrest. The *Examiner* ran the head, "Crime Record of Billings, Dynamiter"—misleading as Billings had been convicted only of transporting dynamite—and gave his name, occupation, age, height and weight; under "Marks or Scars," it noted, "Bullet wound on left thumb." The *Chronicle* headline read, "Suspect Billings Has a Prison Record," with a similar inaccuracy, that he had been sentenced as a "Dynamiter at Sacramento," and printed the same description but with, "Bullet wound across thumb of *right* hand" (emphasis added). That afternoon, the *Bulletin* reported that six people had been arrested: Billings; Edward Nolan, a machinist and friend of Mooney's; Billings's landlady, Mrs. Belle Lavin; Thomas Ryan, a restaurant picket; an unnamed suspect who turned out to be a man named Antone Fedone; and Israel Weinberg. Weinberg was at the wheel of his jitney on Market Street when Draper Hand and an officer named Desmond stopped him, ordered his passengers out and told him that he was under arrest. "What am I arrested for?" asked Weinberg. There being no warrant, Hand said, "I don't know." Weinberg, thinking that this was just another harassment of jitney drivers, was taken to the North End police station. The union card on his machine was taken off and torn up, and he was questioned on and off for two days before being told that he was charged with murder. Weinberg would testify later that Swanson, in an aside, said, "Didn't I tell you I would get you?"

Swanson and some officers went to Mrs. Lavin's boardinghouse, searched Billings's room and confiscated guns, cartridges and some Cadillac ball bearings. They searched Weinberg's home and found nothing remotely incriminating, but they confiscated a receipt from PG&E for the gas bill that Weinberg had paid on Saturday the twenty-second. They broke into Rena Mooney's studio in the Eilers Building and found some cartridges of Mooney's and a notebook of Rena's, which they also confiscated. Late that evening, they raided the basement of Nolan's home and found Mooney's motorcycle, various articles of hardware, clay and Epsom salts.

On Thursday the twenty-seventh, when Billings's picture, his name and the names of the others arrested on Wednesday appeared in the *Chronicle* and the *Examiner*, one Estelle Smith came to the Hall of Justice and was seen by Fickert, Matheson, Cunha, Goff and Brennan. Miss Smith, variously described as a stenographer or nurse in dental parlors at 721 Market Street (a few addresses east of the *Bulletin*), said that she saw Billings at her employer's office shortly after 1:00 p.m. in the afternoon of Saturday the twenty-second. He had come up to the stairs carrying a "black satchel," "grip" or "camera case," depending on the account one read, and had asked if he might go on to the building's roof. She said that he was perspiring and nervous and claimed to be sick from the heat. Miss Smith said that she dampened a towel, wiped the perspiration from his brow and gave him a seat by a window while she asked her employer's permission to let him go up to the roof. She was about to move the case when Billings exclaimed, "My God, girl, don't touch that!" Billings, she said, explained, "I am afraid you will strain the lens in my camera," more calmly. She got her employer's permission to let Billings go up. As he was on the roof, Miss Smith said that another man came up, "rude" and "repulsive-looking," "a Russian Jew or something that way," and tried to force his way up to the roof until a woman came up the steps and called him back. The man and woman, whom Miss Smith later identified as Rena Mooney, left at about 1:47 p.m. Miss Smith said that she looked out the window at the parade, and as Mayor Rolph passed below, she waved a towel

Estelle Smith, circa 1917. *Bancroft Library*.

at him and called, "Hello, Mayor Rolph." Billings, she said, came down from the roof and left about five minutes after that.

Estelle Smith identified Billings in his cell—*not* in a lineup—as the man with the camera case. Hubbard Wade, a schoolteacher from Hawaii who was in the dental parlors at the same time, corroborated her information. Smith would tell the grand jury that she noticed Billings's mashed right thumb "because I have one almost like it on my finger." But Billings's wound was on his left thumb; the *Chronicle* had erroneously reported it on his right. Smith may have been mistaken about which thumb—if she had really seen Billings—or she may have just repeated the *Chronicle*'s report. Significantly, Billings had a conspicuous facial rash, but Smith did not mention it as an identifying factor in her testimony.

Sunny Jim Rolph congratulated Estelle Smith personally for her service to the city, and the *Examiner* commended her editorially: "The type of mind possessed by Miss Estelle Smith, the young woman who has identified Warren K. Billings…is the sort of mind which is of decided value to the world… There are not many who are called upon to serve the State as Miss Smith has been, to act as a witness in a capital trial; but all should develop the power of close observations, of precise memory, as Miss Smith has done."

On Thursday the twenty-seventh, the *Bulletin* quoted Matheson as saying that he had information that Tom and Rena Mooney had left San Francisco on Saturday the twenty-second at 4:00 p.m.—just after the bomb exploded in other words—and Matheson was alleged to have "definite information as to Mooney's whereabouts." Matheson was suggesting that the Mooneys were fugitives from justice, but his statement that they had left San Francisco on Saturday was simply wrong, which Matheson had every reason to know as White had had the Mooneys shadowed by Sergeant McConnell since the previous Monday the twenty-fourth: they left, as they had been planning for a while, to vacation at Montesano on the Russian River, a popular resort area about fifty miles north of San Francisco. The Mooneys bought round-trip tickets and took the ferry to Marin Country and the train to Montesano, where they rented a tent and a rowboat and spent three days on the river.

On Thursday, they rowed downriver to Monte Rio. Rena bought an *Examiner* and was shocked to see the headline:

Billings, Weinberg, Nolan Arrested; Mooneys Escape!

Without changing out of their bathing suits, the Mooneys went to a telegraph office, where Tom sent a telegram to Chief White in San Francisco:

> *Wife and I left San Francisco last Monday 8:45 for week's vacation at Montesano. See by Examiner I am wanted by San Francisco police. My movements are and have been an open book. Will return by next train to San Francisco. I consider this attempt to incriminate me in connection with bomb outrage one of the most dastardly pieces of work ever attempted.*
>
> *Tom Mooney*

Mooney sent a copy of the telegram to Older at the *Bulletin*. The Mooneys left their boat and caught the afternoon train to San Francisco, but at Guerneville, they were arrested by McConnell and other San Francisco officers and taken by several cars via a circuitous route to Sausalito, an unnecessary cloak-and-dagger procedure that resulted in the party's arriving too late to catch the last ferry. A launch had to be chartered for the trip across the bay, and the Mooneys did not arrive in San Francisco until about midnight.

At the Hall of Justice, the Mooneys were separated and searched. Fickert, Swanson, Brennan and others interrogated Tom until about 4:30 a.m. He acknowledged his activities against the URR, his associations and sympathies with radicals and anarchists and his ownership of the motorcycle and other items in Nolan's garage but would not incriminate himself nor anyone else. Separately, both Tom and Rena said that they were in or on the Eilers Building from 1:30 p.m. until 3:00 p.m. on the twenty-second and had witnesses. Mooney demanded to know the charges against him. None, he was told, but he was suspected of murder. Mooney repeatedly insisted on counsel, eighty-six times, but his requests were ignored or evaded. Brennan accused Mooney of being guilty of the bombing and then backed off, saying that he was hiding a connection with the perpetrators. Brennan apparently reasoned that an innocent man did not need counsel; if he did, he had something to hide. Fickert said later that if Mooney had "named some counsel, we would have phoned him." Tom was put in solitary confinement, and Rena slept in the lavatory of the women's quarters on a thin mattress. They were not indicted until August.

On Friday and Saturday after the arrests, Fickert was reported as confident that he would convict the leaders of a "widespread conspiracy" responsible for the bombing. He claimed he had "definite evidence to connect the Mooneys with the recent dynamiting of a United Railroads tower at San Bruno" and suggested that the bomb on July 22 was somehow intended for the URR. He also alleged that "Billings offered to make certain admissions if we would offer a certain degree of compromise. Also one other suspect, a man with a wife and a child stated that he would agree to come through with certain facts if we would accept a proposition [Weinberg and Nolan were both married with a child]. These offers were not accepted in whole or in part."

But other explanations for the bombing appeared. The *Bulletin* reported that Matheson had sent Bunner and another detective to Oakland to look into the bombing a month earlier of the Sixteenth Street Depot in Oakland, across the bay, as "it is suspected that the two crimes may be connected." A connection would threaten or demolish the district attorney's case, as witnesses described three men on the train who could not have been Billings, Mooney or their associates. The *Bulletin* also reported the Mooneys' alibi that they were in and on the Eilers Building, which they said they could prove by witnesses. And there were those troublesome witnesses who saw the men with the suitcase. One thing they all had in common were descriptions that could not by any stretch of the imagination have been of Billings or Mooney. The shorter of the two men was taller than Billings's five feet, four inches; the taller was shorter and lighter than Mooney; and their hair and skin colors were different, particularly in the case of sandy-haired, fair-skinned Billings, with his facial rash.

One way or another, the witnesses were disposed of. William Taylor was put on a boat to Stockton and told to wait until called to testify, which he never was. M.T. Pendergast, the gardener who saw the two men at Steuart Street, was persistent. Even the *Chronicle*, no friend of labor and certainly not of Billings or Mooney, ran a story below a front-page headline, "Oakland Gardener Sees Swarthy Man Place Bomb":

> *Overshadowing all other developments in yesterday's investigation of Saturday's bomb outrage was the positive statement made to the police by M.T. Pendergast…to the effect that he witnessed the placing of the death-dealing suit case at Market and Steuart streets Saturday afternoon, and that the man who left it there was a short, dark and swarthy individual, and did not in the least resemble Warren K. Billings.*

Pendergast stuck so firmly to his account that Fickert smeared him as "part of a plot to divert suspicion from Mooney and Billings." "We were informed," said Fickert (he did not say by whom), "that Pendergast…is a friend of Mooney and an I.W.W. agitator…We threw him out of the office."

On Sunday the thirtieth, the *Examiner* reported a new witness. The itinerant waiter John McDonald, misidentified as a "laborer," had originally described two men whose appearances tallied with those described by Pendergast, even down to the color of the suit on one. McDonald's first identification was in affidavit form, countersigned by Officers George McCullough and Peter Hughes and reported to Matheson, but now he "positively identified Billings and Mooney as two men he had observed near the scene of the crime a few moments before the bomb exploded." Mooney, said McDonald, appeared nervous and repeatedly looked at his watch and the Ferry Building clock. "McDonald," said the *Examiner*, "is considered a witness of outstanding importance by Fickert and Captain Duncan Matheson of the police bomb bureau." The affidavit disappeared for years, its existence unknown. With McDonald and Smith as primary witnesses, Fickert announced that he would ask the grand jury for premeditated murder indictments against Billings, the Mooneys and Edward Nolan, with charges to follow against Weinberg. Mrs. Lavin and the others were released.

The constitutions of the United States (Fourth Amendment of the Bill of Rights) and the State of California prohibit unreasonable searches and seizures. A warrant for search shall be issued only "upon probable cause, supported by oath or affirmation, particularly describing the place to be searched and the persons and things to be seized." Disregarding constitutional protections, Fickert, Cunha, Bunner, Swanson and others raided the homes of Nolan, Weinberg and Mrs. Lavin without warrants. A warrant was issued for the search of Rena Mooney's studio, but even that search was illegal as no return was filed with the magistrate.

The arrests were illegal. The California Penal Code (Section 836) specified that an officer may arrest for a felony not committed in the officer's presence, without a warrant, when the officer "has reasonable cause for believing the person arrested to have committed it." Even if the searches of the residences of Billings, Mooney and the others had been legal, rather than fishing expeditions, no evidence was found to link them with the bombing, and there was no reasonable cause for arrest, warrant or no. Some of the witnesses who had seen the men on the street on July 22 were shown photographs of Billings and Mooney, among others, but no witnesses prior to the arrests identified the men as Billings and/or Mooney. The only "witnesses" who did identify them were McDonald and Smith, and only *after* pictures of Billings and Mooney appeared in the newspapers. Had anyone identified Mooney, for instance, before his picture appeared, McConnell would have had cause to arrest him immediately instead of shadowing him at the Russian River until Thursday.

Section 849 of the California Penal Code stated, "When an arrest is made without a warrant by a peace officer or private person, the person arrested must, without unnecessary delay, be taken before the nearest or most accessible magistrate in the county in which the arrest is made, and an information, stating the charge against the person, must be laid before such magistrate." Section 825 stated that any attorney licensed in California may visit the arrested person and that any officer "who willfully refuses or neglects to allow such attorney to visit a prisoner is guilty of a misdemeanor." At Mooney's trial, defense attorney Bourke Cockran asked Matheson on the stand, "You knew that, the man having been arrested without a warrant, you were at once to take him before a magistrate?"

"Yes, I am familiar with that section of the code," said Matheson.

"Why didn't you do it?"

"In the interests of justice."

"In the interests of justice you suspended law?"

"Yes, sir."

The backward process went hand in glove with the reward offer by the Law and Order Committee, which noted, "Recent disturbances on the waterfront were accompanied by violence...The spirit of lawlessness in the community logically terminated in the damnable outrage of Saturday [July 22]." It was an invitation to reward-hunters to incriminate strikers for the bombing, even by perjury.

Just after the arrests, Martin Swanson saw attorney Maxwell McNutt outside McNutt's office at 110 Sutter Street and asked him what he was thinking.

"I think there is too much Swanson," McNutt answered. "It is very evident to me that the arrest of these defendants was caused by yourself." McNutt reminded Swanson that after Mooney was acquitted in Martinez, Detective Barrett said, "Well, Mac, you get Mooney out of this but we put a red shirt on him

Defense attorney Maxwell McNutt, circa 1917. *San Francisco Public Library History Room.*

and we will get something on him some day." Swanson remembered. McNutt added, "Martin, you are the man who caused the arrest of these defendants, and the identification is being sought afterwards."

Swanson conceded that and asked McNutt, "Do you think if we keep private detectives in the background and make the public believe that the district attorney and the police are prosecuting these cases that we won't get them?"

"Not if anybody is awake, you won't," McNutt shot back.

"You won't take the case?" asked Swanson.

"I am beginning to get interested," McNutt replied.

Trials

On August 1, the grand jury indicted Billings, the Mooneys, Nolan and Weinberg for murder. Billings went to trial first, on Monday September 11, before Judge Dunne, for the murder of Mrs. Van Loo. A jury was sworn on Tuesday, but selection was questionable. Women did not yet serve, and jury lists consisted mostly of elderly men—pensioners, retired shopkeepers and saloonkeepers wanting to pick up a few dollars and free lunches. The *Bulletin* noted, "It is a curious fact that of the twelve jurors sworn, nine are 'retired' business men, and that of those rejected, many were also on the 'retired' list." (Foreman Hugh Frazer was eighty-three.) Repeat jurors such as these had a reputation for voting for convictions, as prosecutions were always conducted by the district attorney, and defense attorneys varied.

The prosecution's strategy in Billings's case was to appeal to inflamed public opinion and blame the killings on the "vast conspiracy" that Fickert associated with the defendants. As Billings had been convicted of transporting dynamite, his position was weaker than Mooney's, and his conviction would, in turn, help convict Mooney. The prosecution showed picture after picture of blasted, bloody bodies on Steuart Street until press, spectators and jury were sick. It harped on Billings's dynamite conviction in Sacramento until Dunne ruled that inadmissible since Billings was on trial for murder, not conspiracy. The prosecution then produced a case containing forty-six sticks of dynamite with which Billings allegedly had planned to bomb utility towers near the Tanforan Racetrack in San Bruno, but Dunne also ruled that inadmissible.

On Friday the fifteenth, two surprise prosecution witnesses appeared. Mrs. Mellie Edeau, a widowed seamstress who lived with her daughter, Sadie, in Oakland, had told co-workers she was at Steuart Street on July 22 and saw "two middle-aged men, one of whom carried a square black suitcase with metal trimmings" before the bomb exploded. At the urging of a co-worker, she told Oakland police chief Walter Peterson about the men and said that she wanted to go to San Francisco to identify the suspects. Accompanied by Oakland inspector William Smith, Mrs. Edeau was shown Billings and Mooney in their cells by Goff—again, there was no lineup—but told Smith, "I have never seen either of these men in my life." The same day, daughter Sadie told Inspector Smith that she had not seen anything at Steuart and was not interested in the case. Mrs. Edeau told her co-workers afterward that Billings was "nothing but a kid" and that "Mooney was rather a sullen-looking fellow" but that she had never seen him before.

The Edeaus did not testify before the grand jury, but at trial, they said something completely different from what they had told Inspector Smith. Questioned by Fickert, Mrs. Edeau said that she saw Billings with a suitcase on the roof of 721 Market and saw him come down afterward and talk with a man and woman on the sidewalk at around 1:30 p.m. She did not mention being at Steuart Street at all. Daughter Sadie corroborated her.

Estelle Smith repeated her story of seeing Billings go onto the roof of 721 Market with some kind of case and, like the Edeaus, said that he came down at about 1:30 p.m. and went east down Market (toward Steuart). But Smith had told the grand jury that she had asked her mother, Mrs. Alice Kidwell, who was in the dental parlors on July 22, to tell her when the parade came by so she could watch from the window. Billings, she said, left about five minutes later. One R.C. Saunders took a photograph from across Market showing someone waving a towel at Rolph from a window of 721 Market. A street clock in the photograph showed the time as 1:50 p.m.; Billings would have been at the spot until about 1:55 p.m. (if he was there at all). McNutt said confidently, "The more witnesses they find to say that Billings was at 721 Market Street, the better we like it. They are proving an alibi for Billings." (See photo on page 71.)

On Monday the eighteenth, John McDonald, the prosecution's star witness, repeated his grand jury testimony that he had seen Billings at Steuart Street between 1:50 p.m. and 2:00 p.m. with the fatal suitcase. His story was completely incompatible with the accounts of Estelle Smith, the Edeaus and the defense witnesses. According to McDonald, Billings came north up the west side of Steuart Street "about eight minutes to two," looking from right

The arrow at upper left points to the clock outside Sorensen's Jewelers, 715 Market Street, showing 1:50 p.m. as Mayor Rolph marches by. Estelle Smith said that Billings would be in her building until five minutes later. *San Francisco Public Library History Room.*

to left "as though his head were on a pivot," put the suitcase down, spoke to Mooney and continued to Market. For Billings to have come up from Mission, he would have had to go south down one of the streets intersecting Market, a distance of about five hundred feet; walk east on Mission to Steuart, more than four thousand feet; and come back up Steuart to Market, almost another five hundred feet. Even if Billings had left 721 Market just after Rolph passed, as Smith said, and had arrived at Steuart at 2:00 p.m., the very last minute allowed by McDonald's testimony, he would have had to run more than five thousand feet along crowded sidewalks in ten minutes. Billings, moreover, would have been carrying a suitcase that according to the prosecution contained 30 pounds of dynamite—and Billings weighed only 124 pounds. (See map on page 72.)

McNutt's strategy was to discredit the testimony of Smith and others who claimed to have seen Billings at 721 Market, as well as of McDonald; to have Billings testify, with corroboration, that he was nowhere near Steuart

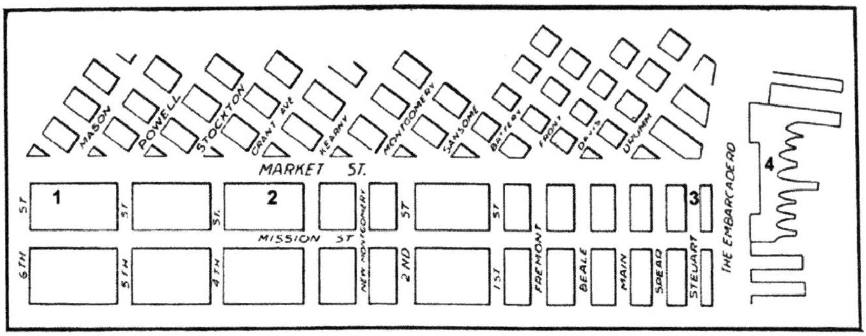

|← 721 Market Street to Steuart, 4,066 feet →|

|← 975 Market Street to Steuart, 6,088 feet →|

1. Eilers Building, 975 Market Street, where the Mooneys were photographed on the roof at 2:01 p.m.
2. 721 Market Street, where Estelle Smith claimed she saw Billings about 1:55 p.m.
3. Steuart Street below Market, where the bomb exploded at 2:06 p.m. John McDonald claimed he saw Billings and Mooney with a suitcase there, also about 1:55 p.m.
4. Ferry Building.

Market Street between the Embarcadero and Sixth, July 22, 1916. *Map by author.*

Street; and to show that while a suitcase may have been on the Steuart Street sidewalk, the bomb was a percussion bomb thrown from a roof, destroying the suitcase at the same time it killed Mrs. Van Loo and others. The last point echoed the *Bulletin*'s report on Saturday, July 22, of a thrown bomb. On Tuesday the nineteenth, four men who were on the roof of 721 Market watching the parade from 1:30 p.m. to 4:00 p.m. testified that Billings was not with them. Additionally, witness Al de Caccia of Oakland, who resembled Billings, had been standing with one leg up on the edge of the roof looking down on Market. The *Bulletin* printed a picture of De Caccia in profile, with Billings in profile below. The resemblance is convincing.

Billings gave a good account of his movements on the afternoon of July 22, including the streets he crossed, the parade divisions on side streets and a conversation he overheard between a woman in charge of a girls' parade division and a man at Grant and Union Square Avenues. He also described Dr. Patek's Hudson, with the white scratch, on Union Square Avenue (he did not say he put the scratch on it himself). Several witnesses corroborated him. M.T. Pendergast, the thorn in the side of the prosecution, repeated his testimony about the dark-suited man placing the suitcase on the Steuart Street sidewalk at about 1:15 p.m. And Dr. J. Mora Moss of Oakland, who marched, testified that he saw "a dark, cylindrical object," apparently hurled from a roof, that exploded when it hit the ground. Other witnesses testified similarly, but as Ernest Hopkins observed, the flash and shock of an explosion can leave a lingering image on the retina, suggesting that something was there before when it actually happened afterward.

Acquittal seemed likely. The *Chronicle* ran a headline, "Billings' Evidence Is a Jolt to State," with a subhead, "His Account Is Borne Out by Many Credible Witnesses Who Make It Appear that He Was Not Near Explosion." By Thursday, the *Bulletin* was firmly on Billings's side. With the witnesses who saw the suitcase on Steuart before Billings supposedly arrived, the witnesses who corroborated his account of his movements on Saturday the twenty-second, "Billings's double" De Caccia on the roof of 721 Market and the thrown-bomb witnesses, there was more than enough reasonable doubt about the prosecution's case.

Final arguments began on Thursday the twenty-first. McNutt asked why Billings should have taken a time bomb to the roof of 721 Market if he was going to take it to Steuart Street later, which the prosecution never did explain. He criticized Swanson's involvement:

> *This historic theory, formed in the brain of private detective Martin Swanson, hatched in the superheated, perfervid imagination of the Estelle Smiths, the McDonalds, and reared to maturity by the Fickerts, the Brennans and the traffic squad—God save the mark…They picked out the easiest man to convict, then went out and hunted up evidence that might apply to him.*
>
> *Tell me if McDonald, on the further side of Steuart Street, with a crowd in front of him, could see a five-foot-four-inch man going through the antics he describes? Let us leave poor McDonald to his drugstore dreams…*
>
> *This case will go down in history as a monument to egregious stupidity and incapacity.*

Fickert gave the first address for the state. Vituperative rather than legal, he snarled:

> *Place this fiend where never again he can repeat this act! Say to him, and to all the anarchistic breed, "You cannot get by with that stuff—we are going to have law and order here"…This American flag, this American flag was what they desired to offend! They offended that, by killing the women and children who worshipped it. Here is another photograph of Mrs. Van Loo,*

> *dying on the streets of our city, and in a feeble hand she holds the American flag, and if that flag is to continue to wave, you men must put an end to such acts as these!*

Fickert asked for the death penalty.

Brennan followed, but with a surprising difference. Billings, he said, was agent, not principal, "a puppet for others," and his conviction would lead to a confession implicating the bombing's mastermind. "Gentlemen of the jury, I believe you will reach such a verdict as will enable this young man to do this right thing in this case." Brennan then asked for a verdict of guilty of murder in the first degree, with a penalty of life imprisonment. Hopkins couldn't believe his ears: life imprisonment for the crime that had caused ten deaths!

Dunne continued the case until Saturday the twenty-third. The jury heard instructions and retired just before 11:00 a.m. As usual, the press took a twenty-five-cent pool, the bets running almost unanimously for a hung jury. In fact, the jury reached a verdict after three ballots and about two hours, went to lunch at state expense, met again to agree on a sentence and returned just before 3:00 p.m. The bailiff had warned that any demonstration would bring arrest, but it was unnecessary. "We, the jury," read Foreman Frazer to a hushed courtroom, "find the defendant Warren K. Billings guilty of murder of the first degree and we hereby fix the punishment at imprisonment in the state prison of the state of California for life." Press and public were stunned. *Bulletin* editor Frank Sheridan had a heart attack.

On the Tuesday after the verdict, the *Bulletin* printed Billings's response. Billings had little formal education but showed himself capable of concise eloquence (emphasis original):

> *The verdict that was rendered against me is, in my consideration, one of the most atrocious outrages in the annals of criminal procedure; and I wish to attract the attention of the court to the fact that* **that verdict was just exactly what the Assistant District Attorney asked for, and nothing else**. *Not only did the evidence presented here tend to create a reasonable doubt in the minds of all fair-minded and unprejudiced men, but it did also create such doubt in the minds of the jury, or they would not have brought in the verdict carrying with it life imprisonment. The perpetrator of that dastardly crime could deserve nothing less than capital punishment; and, as a firm believer in American justice, I say that those twelve men have not done their duty as citizens of these United States and of this city by bringing such a verdict.*

This verdict is not only an outrage against an innocent man, but is also an outrage against civilization and progress, inasmuch as it would give me a chance, if I were guilty, to involve in this serious trouble all those against whom I might bear any malice. This, I think you will concede, is a very dangerous arrangement of affairs; for, if I were guilty of the offense with which I am charged, would I not be liable to involve the innocent as well as the guilty? But…the evidence in this case is such that no man with an ounce of fairness in his make-up could conceive of such a verdict as was rendered here.

Almost immediately after Billings's conviction, new information appeared, on the basis of which McNutt would ask for a retrial. D.J. Kidwell, the husband of Mrs. Alice Kidwell, Estelle Smith's mother, was serving a two-year sentence in Folsom Prison for forgery committed in Ventura County. McNutt made public a letter from Alice to her husband, dated September 2 and saying in part:

The authorities are going to get you out—maybe in a few days—and maybe by the 16th; have got work for you in the Union Iron Works, anyway at $4 day—maybe more. Captain Matterson [sic] *and the District Attorney went to see two of the board this A.M. and will see the others at Sacramento… Do not delay, for we expect to have a private meeting to get you out.*

Assistant DA Brennan, who had recommended life imprisonment for Billings, admitted that he had interested himself in Kidwell's parole application but did so purely to provide Mrs. Kidwell with a means of support while she waited in San Francisco to testify. "As it looked as though we would need her until after the first of the year, this looked like a way to help her out…I thought I could get work for [her husband]." Folsom Prison director Henry Eickhoff, however, said that Kidwell's parole would be heard in the usual way. It was on the October calendar, he added, too late for action in September, and in any case, "[n]either Captain Matheson, Fickert nor anyone else could influence the board."

Witnesses William Taylor and Elmer Kimberlin came forward with their descriptions of the man they saw put down the suitcase on Steuart Street. The testimony of Louis Rominger, a prosecution witness who had corroborated Estelle Smith's story, was impeached by W.C. Kerch, a businessman whose office in the Camm Building overlooked the roof of 721 Market Street. Rominger testified that he had helped Billings get his heavy case up through a light well to the roof, but Kerch had seen the whole thing and said that the man with the case was about five-foot-nine and did not resemble Billings. Kerch and Rominger went to the North End Police Station to identify Billings after his arrest, and both said that Billings was not the man on the roof. Kerch told Estelle Smith, "You had better forget about the reward. I and Rominger cannot identify Billings as the man," but Smith said, "That doesn't make any difference. There are fifty others who can and will identify him." Kerch was subpoenaed as a prosecution witness but was not called to the stand. Rominger was also subpoenaed and was called, and to Kerch's amazement, he testified that he saw Billings on the roof. Assistant District Attorney Harry McKenzie would sign an affidavit admitting that Kerch and Rominger had, in fact, failed to identify Billings, which put the prosecution in the position of using perjured testimony to convict. But Dunne saw no merit in the new findings, denied the retrial motion and, on October 7, 1916, sentenced Billings to life imprisonment.

The defense revealed remarkable things about Estelle Smith. Originally from Kentucky, she and her uncle had been indicted in Los Angeles in 1913 for the murder of a chorus girl with whom Estelle's lover, her half-brother, Morris Bohannon, had become involved. Estelle and her uncle were confronting the pair when a gun went off, killing the girl. Estelle's uncle alone was convicted, of second-degree murder, and was sentenced to twelve years in San Quentin, but it was suspected that he was taking the rap for Estelle. A year later, Estelle was arrested in Los Angeles for prostitution and forfeited bail. She would also say in an affidavit that she was addicted to morphine in July 1916, even taking it during Billings's trial recess. The prosecution did not call her for Mooney's trial.

On Monday, August 21, 1916, the Mooneys entered not guilty pleas. Tom's case was continued until January because of the Christmas holidays. The IWDL and Alexander Berkman had appealed to eastern labor leaders for help, and Mooney's case came to the attention of lawyer and former New York congressman W. Bourke Cockran, one of the most famous orators in the country. He was reluctant to get involved at first, but after reading a transcript of the Billings trial, he became convinced that a travesty of justice had taken place and volunteered to defend Mooney without fee. Cockran conferred prestige on the defense, but he was not an experienced criminal lawyer and left most of the legal work to McNutt and others.

Mooney's trial began on Wednesday, January 3, 1917, before Judge Franklin Griffin, a Progressive who had been Hiram Johnson's executive secretary. The previous Saturday, December 30, Cunha, Swanson, Draper Hand and Detective Michael Burke raided the offices of the *Blast*, purportedly to find evidence that the Preparedness Day bomb plot had been hatched there. They found none but seized mailing lists, cartoons, files and personal letters of Assistant Editor Eleanor Fitzgerald. When she resisted, saying that her letters were none of their business, Hand grabbed her by the wrists, inflicting bruises. She showed the bruises to Griffin's court and accused the DA's office of trying to stir up prejudice against Mooney and the other defendants. A warrant had been issued, but Cockran said that the raid was illegal, as no return was filed with the issuing magistrate, and added that making the letters public was a violation of law. Besides, no gentleman would do such a thing. Cunha said, "As long as I am identified with the District Attorney's office, when crimes as horrible as this are committed, I shall go the limit in my investigations. I shall use all my legal authority, and, if necessary, I hope I shall have the backbone to exceed my authority in order to stamp out this class of crime." Griffin rebuked him: "Mr. Cunha, I don't propose to permit that kind of language to be used in my court. Thomas J. Mooney is the same, in the eyes of this court, as any other defendant, and such an attitude as you express is utterly irregular, uncalled for and out of order."

Judge Franklin Griffin, circa 1917. *From* The Survey, *July 7, 1917.*

Jury selection took two weeks, many veniremen being excused for bias. The panel was sworn on Thursday the eighteenth and included several retirees—including an elderly graybeard who fell asleep once during the proceedings—but was generally more representative of San Francisco's population than Billings's jury. Foreman William MacNevin, however, was a personal friend of Cunha's, but that would not be made public until after the trial. Cunha, young and unknown outside California, saw the opportunity for advancement in opposing a national figure like Cockran and opened the prosecution's case with a sweeping allegation that Mooney, Berkman and anarchists generally

Assistant District Attorney Edward Cunha, circa 1917. *Author's collection.*

had planned not just the Preparedness Day bombing but also an uprising against the governments of the State of California and the United States, with assassinations of Governor Hiram Johnson and President Woodrow Wilson thrown in for good measure.

The connection of Mooney and Billings with anarchism was tenuous. Mooney had written just one article for the *Blast*, and Billings had simply met Mooney at its offices. Cockran ridiculed the notion that Mooney's socialist beliefs were the same thing as anarchistic ones—in fact, the two were diametrically opposed: socialism advocated governmental control of industry and distribution of commodities, while anarchism "is a conception of human nature so lofty that it assumes all men are inherently good, and therefore if left free from coercion by government would spontaneously organize a society free from crime, where all could voluntarily cooperate in production and divide the fruits of their industry in peace and justice." (See photos on pages 79 and 80.)

Invective notwithstanding, the defense built a strong case in the first week. Before Billings's trial, McNutt had learned about Wade Hamilton's photographs showing the Mooneys on the Eilers Building roof watching the parade. Sensing the importance of the photos, Hamilton gave the negatives and a set of prints to Fickert and kept a set of prints himself. Without further explanation, Fickert claimed that the pictures disproved the Mooneys' alibi. McNutt demanded to see them and was given the runaround and then told that the films had been destroyed. He threatened legal action and was finally given a blurred set of prints by Blum, the police photographer, which in spite of poor quality seemed to show Rolph passing below the building, making the time about 2:00 p.m. In court, McNutt demanded the negatives, and Griffin ordered, "Go and get Mr. Blum and tell him to deliver the films which were delivered to him a week after the Preparedness Parade." The negatives were given to the

Roof of the Eilers Building, 973 Market. **1:** Tom Mooney; **2:** Rena Mooney (holding hat); **3:** street clock; and **4:** Flood Building, Powell and Market. The Ferry Building is just visible in the distant upper right. *San Francisco Public Library History Room.*

defense, and in Blum's presence, handwriting and photographic expert Theodore Kytka enlarged successive prints in which a street clock showed 1:58 p.m., 2:01 p.m. and 2:04 p.m. The Eilers Building being more than six thousand feet west of Steuart Street, McDonald's seeing Mooney on Steuart with the suitcase at 1:50 p.m. or later was impossible.

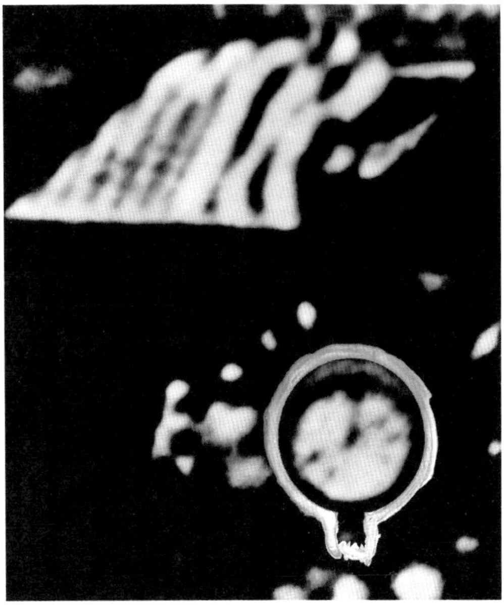

Street clock, enlarged, shows one minute past 2:00 p.m. John McDonald testified at Billings's trial that he saw Billings and Mooney just before 2:00 p.m. at Steuart Street, more than a mile east. *San Francisco Public Library History Room.*

Prosecution witness John McDonald, who testified seeing Billings and Mooney on Steuart Street at 1:50 p.m. during Billings's trial and then changed the time to 1:30 p.m. at Mooney's trial. *Bancroft Library.*

The prosecution claimed that the bomb was a time bomb that Mooney left at Steuart Street, after which he went to the Eilers Building, where he and Rena were photographed. Anticipating this, McNutt called several witnesses to corroborate the Mooneys' testimony that they were in or on the building between 11:30 a.m. and 3:00 p.m. (no clock parts from a time bomb were found anyway). On Thursday the twenty-fifth, Cockran put McDonald on the stand. McDonald had testified at Billings's trial that he saw Billings and Mooney there between 1:50 p.m. and 2:00 p.m., but now he said that he saw them at about 1:45 p.m., which, conveniently for the prosecution, would have given Mooney time to get back to the Eilers Building roof. Cockran nailed the contradictions, and McDonald reverted to his original testimony, saying that he had seen Billings and Mooney at 2:00 p.m. With the photographs, witnesses at the Eilers Building and the unreliable McDonald as prosecution witness, the defense's case was ironclad. "Few better alibis," said Hopkins, "have ever been advanced."

ON FRIDAY THE TWENTY-SIXTH, the prosecution called a new witness, a man kept secret by the prosecution and unknown to press, public and the defense. It was Frank C. Oxman, a sixty-two-year-old cattle and sheep rancher of Durkee, eastern Oregon, an expansive, sparsely settled region. Oxman was large, tall, white-haired and sun-browned, and he spoke artlessly and deliberately.

On the stand, Oxman said that he had arrived in San Francisco by train from Willows, California, about 130 miles north, on Saturday, July 22, and had registered at the Terminal Hotel, on the north side of Market just opposite the intersection of Steuart. He was at Steuart and Market Streets looking for a place to eat when he saw a Ford jitney coming east down the block with a man in the front passenger seat holding a suitcase on the running board.

"Can you identify Thomas J. Mooney as one of the men who was in the automobile?" asked Cunha.

Pointing to Mooney, Oxman answered, "I do not know Mooney by name, but that is the man sitting there." Cunha asked Oxman if he recognized anyone else. "Yes," said Oxman, pointing to Billings, "that auburn-haired young man sitting over there."

"Did you recognize anyone else?" asked Cunha.

"Yes, that man sitting beside Billings."

"You mean the defendant, Israel Weinberg?"

"Yes."

"Now, did you see anyone else in the automobile?"

"Yes. I saw Mrs. Mooney." The courtroom was deadly quiet as Oxman continued, saying that there was a fifth person, a foreign-looking man with a stubby mustache, not present in the room. He said that the car stopped at Steuart Street, and Billings got out, rudely brushing Oxman aside. "Don't you think you're a pretty small boy to be jostling a fat man like me?" Oxman said he asked Billings. He said Billings took the suitcase from the running board and handed it to the man with the mustache, who had also gotten out. Oxman said that the man took it down Steuart Street toward Mission and placed it down a little distance beyond the saloon. Billings caught up with him, took the suitcase back to the saloon and put it on the sidewalk. Mooney had gotten out of the car and was looking at his watch and the clock on the Ferry Building. Billings and the third man rejoined him, and Oxman said that he heard Mooney say, "Give it to him—the bulls may be here any moment." Billings gave something, presumably money, to the third man, who disappeared into the crowd. Billings and Mooney got back in the car, and Weinberg drove down Steuart Street toward Mission. Oxman drew a diagram of the car's and the defendants' movements.

Oxman said that all the places to eat were packed, and he had bought fruit at a stand. At about 1:45 p.m., he crossed Market Street, munching it on his way back to the Terminal Hotel, where he was waiting for a business telephone call when the bomb went off. "I remembered the incident in a general way because of my own narrow escape from the explosion."

Cunha said, "That is all," and told the defense that it could have the witness.

The courtroom was stunned, the defense table particularly. Cockran was taken aback like everyone else but began cross-examination: "Could you not be mistaken in your identification of all these persons?"

"Absolutely no," said Oxman, "I am certain they are the same people." Upon further cross-examination, he said that he was taken to the county jail of his own volition and identified the defendants there. Pressed by Cockran as to what Mrs. Mooney was wearing on July 22, Oxman said he had only a vague idea what she was hearing—perhaps a gray hat with a red band—but he wasn't sure.

Frank Oxman on the witness stand sketches his version of Billings and Mooney leaving the suitcase at Steuart Street. *Inset*: Jimmy McDougall, who sat on the suitcase. *From the* Examiner, *January 27, 1917.*

"Now you mean to tell this jury on your oath, Mr. Oxman, that after seeing these people but once and giving them a single glance you are absolutely sure in your identification of them?"

"Yes, but I didn't say I gave them only one glance." Cockran pressed Oxman about what attracted his attention to the party in the Ford. Oxman said that he thought they were thieves who had stolen the suitcase, emptied it and were trying to get rid of it. He had no memory for details of dress, such as what Mrs. Mooney was wearing, but in his business as a cattleman, he met a lot of faces and had cultivated a memory for them. "I have seen you for the first time for instance, Mr. Cockran, and would be able to identify you a year from now, but I might not be able to tell the clothes you wore when I saw you in court."

Cockran pressed Oxman for details—how long the car was at the corner and whether, as he suspected robbery, he had notified a policeman. Oxman said that the car waited about a minute and a half and that he hadn't seen a policeman on foot, only a mounted one on Market Street. Cockran pressed him further: "You saw a mounted policeman in the middle of the street?"

"Yes, sir."

"You are an honest man, and yet you did not call a policeman?" No, Oxman repeated, he did not called a policeman, but he had taken the precaution of writing down the car's license number. "Oh, you took down the number of the machine, did you," said Cockran, falling into the trap. "Where is it? Do you have it now?"

"Yes, I put it down on the back of a telegram with a notation," said Oxman. Reaching into his breast pocket, he withdrew an envelope from a business telegram. "Here it is." Cockran adjusted his glasses and read:

Ford no. 5187
think stolen grip
S.F. July 22

It was the number of Israel Weinberg's jitney. There was a stir in court. Weinberg whispered audibly that the police could have given the number to Oxman. Cockran was on the spot: "You say you put this notation down immediately. Why did you do that?"

"Because as a cattleman I often have occasion to take the number of machines that figure in raids or in thefts of stock. This is a well-established custom on the range, and I followed it when I saw this automobile drive off. I thought the number of the machine, containing, as I supposed, thieves, might come in handy for the police in connection with some robbery."

Cockran kept trying: "You say that this automobile came down Market Street and that it stopped at the corner of Market and Steuart streets for a few minutes, and that it then continued on down into Steuart Street."

"Yes, sir."

"And don't you know that the parade was moving at that time?"

"I believe it was."

"And do you mean to tell this jury that that automobile was permitted to come down Market Street while the parade was moving?"

"Well, it came down Market Street just the same."

"And that is just as true as anything else you have testified to?"

"Yes, it is."

"That's all," said Cockran.

Oxman caused a huge sensation in what had been a relatively predictable trial. The prosecution gloated that he was "the man whose testimony will hang Mooney." The *Bulletin* headlined, "New Proof Against Mooney" and noted that Oxman gave "startling evidence." The *Examiner* ran a headline, "Rancher Shatters Defense in Bomb Trial," with the subhead, "Cockran Unable to Break Down Testimony After Two Hours of Grueling Cross-Examination; Recital Thrills Court Crowds." It depicted Oxman as the prosecution would have wanted, a reluctant witness who had testified at personal expense out of a sense of duty: "I would have much preferred not to have been a witness in this or any similar trial." Besides his business concerns in Oregon, Oxman's wife was ill. Cockran asked the court to instruct Oxman to remain within its jurisdiction, and Oxman affirmed that he would unless called home to attend to his wife, in which case "all the courts in California could not hold me here."

All major newspapers accepted Oxman's testimony. Provincialism undoubtedly played a part. San Francisco, for all its sophistication, is a western city and could beam with pride when a good old boy westerner, the "honest cattleman" Oxman, bested the great New York lawyer Cockran. The telegram blank, drawn from Oxman's pocket with Weinberg's license number, was a piece of theater to throw Cockran off his guard, and it worked. What the newspapers did not say was that Oxman's story was preposterous. Cockran touched on this, but only briefly, when he asked Oxman how a jitney bus with five people could have come down Market Street, which Oxman dismissed with, "It came down Market Street just the same." That would have been impossible. All motor vehicles other than ambulances, such as the one sent for Adam Fox, and police cars were diverted to Mission, and intersections were roped off. Parade divisions filled the breadth of Market, the sidewalks were eight deep with spectators and there were police at every intersection. Weinberg's jitney, according to Oxman, would have squeezed east all by itself along a narrow stretch of pavement in front of spectators and policeman, as Tom Mooney, the most conspicuous "labor agitator" in San Francisco, one arm out the window, held a suitcase on the running board in the face of a parade coming west up Market…and nobody but Oxman saw

The Ferry Building clock shows 1:45 p.m. as the Preparedness parade moves up Market Street. Oxman said that Weinberg's jitney came down the narrow strip of pavement, *right*, between marchers and spectators, but no picture showed it. *San Francisco Public Library History Room.*

him? The prosecution should have been able to produce not just Oxman, but several, even several hundred, other witnesses—a policeman would have been dandy—but it didn't. Finally, Swanson had grudges against Billings, Mooney and Weinberg and had at least one, possibly all, shadowed, but none of Swanson's operatives testified to seeing Weinberg's jitney with five people on Market Street or Billings and the third man putting the suitcase on the Steuart Street sidewalk while Mooney checked his watch. That wasn't because they didn't want the reward. They would have wanted the reward, but even Swanson's men knew better than to testify to seeing what they hadn't. (See photo above.)

Mooney's trial lasted two more weeks. On Monday, January 29, Sadie Edeau testified for the prosecution. Again contradicting what she and her mother had told Oakland officer Smith, she said that they saw Billings with the suitcase at 721 Market Street on July 22 and added that she saw him with the Mooneys on the sidewalk, after which all three walked down Market. She also said that a man cranked the engine of an automobile at the curb and drove down Market toward the Ferry Building. Asked by Fickert if the man she saw in the automobile was in the courtroom, Sadie Edeau pointed to Israel Weinberg and said, "That is the man." Contradicting herself further, Miss Edeau said that she and her mother identified all the prisoners except Edward Nolan at the county jail. The prosecution's case was essentially finished by Wednesday, other than a vague reference to a witness who would corroborate Oxman's testimony. As the *Bulletin* reported, it was said that there was "a man who was with Oxman at the time" Oxman saw Weinberg's jitney, but such a witness never appeared.

On Friday, February 2, the Mooneys testified, repeating their accounts of being in or on the Eilers Building on July 22. Their stories corroborated each other's, other witnesses corroborated them and the Hamilton photographs were produced. Defense witness R.M. Wood of Oakland testified that he was at Market and Steuart from 1:30 p.m. until the time of the explosion, at practically the same spot where Oxman said he saw Weinberg's jitney, and saw neither a jitney nor any other vehicle except a press car and an official car.

Fickert began final arguments for the prosecution on Wednesday, February 7. As with Billings, he stressed Mooney's reputation and links with radicals,

The Mooneys at Tom's trial. *Left to right*: Rena, Tom and Tom's mother, Mrs. Anna Mooney. *Author's collection.*

including the *Los Angeles Times* bombers. Cockran repeatedly objected, and Judge Griffin cautioned Fickert to confine himself to the present case and told the jury to disregard his remarks. Fickert pitched a contrast between his humble self and the eloquent Cockran: "I have been unable to bring into this court a carefully prepared address replete with literary and oratorical gems to charm the jury and astound posterity. Nor am I endowed with that gift of eloquence 'that can raise the mortal to the skies or drag an angel down,' but in my humble way I shall speak in behalf of the people of the State of California in language as simple as my belief is in the guilt of the defendant." He pleaded for sympathy for the ten bombing victims and vengeance for their murders. Fickert's disavowal of eloquence notwithstanding, he concluded:

> *For, with conscience satisfied with the discharge of duty, no consequence can harm you. There is no evil that we cannot face or fly from but the consciousness of duty disregarded. A sense of duty pursues us ever. It is omnipresent like the deity. If we take to ourselves the wings of morning and dwell in the uttermost parts of the earth, duty performed or duty violated is still with us for our happiness or misery, and if we say darkness shall overcome us, in darkness as in light our obligations are yet with us. We cannot escape their power nor fly from their presence. They are with us in this life, will be with us at the close, and in that scene of inconceivable solemnity which lies yet further onward, and when the memory of Mrs. Knapp has gone we shall still find ourselves surrounded by consciousness of duty to pain us wherever it has been violated and to console us so far as God has given us grace to perform it.*

If that speech sounds too eloquent to have been written by Fickert, it's because it wasn't. In 1830, Massachusetts senator Daniel Webster assisted the prosecution in a celebrated trial of two brothers named Knapp for the murder in Salem of wealthy eighty-two-year-old Captain Joseph White, bludgeoned and stabbed to death in his home. Webster told the jury, "With consciences satisfied with the discharge of duty, no consequences can harm you. There is no evil that we cannot either face or fly from but the consciousness of duty disregarded. A sense of duty pursues us ever. It is omnipresent, like the Deity. If we take to ourselves the wings of the morning, and dwell in the uttermost parts of the sea [*sic*], duty performed, or duty violated, is still with us…" And so on. The only difference was Fickert's insertion of Mrs. Knapp, which interrupted Webster's flow. With sarcasm that might have been evident even to Fickert, the *Bulletin*'s front page reported, "Fickert's Oratory Strangely

Like That of Daniel Webster" and reprinted their addresses in parallel columns, saying:

> *A remarkable case of two great minds running in the same channel came to light today in the trial of Thomas Mooney.*
>
> *The two minds are those of District Attorney Charles M. Fickert and Daniel Webster.*
>
> *Webster was a man honored in his day to the ends of the nation for his eloquence in oratory. Those who read Fickert's speech to the jury delivered in court this morning are now wondering whether he aspires to similar fame.*

McNutt followed for the defense. He stressed Swanson's involvement and ridiculed Oxman's testimony. On Thursday, February 8, Bourke Cockran spoke. The courtroom, reported the *Bulletin*, was "crowded to suffocation." "Society women, labor leaders, members of the Board of Supervisors and other officials, kings of finance, social workers of all types, leaders of clubdom, priests, lawyers and magistrates, and the rank and file of courtroom onlookers jostled each other in the throng." It was a who's who from San Francisco and environs. Cockran spoke deliberately and unemotionally, with references from literature, physics, history, psychology and religion. He treated Fickert and Cunha with delicate sarcasm, saying that they had established no motive for Mooney's committing the crime—indeed, he had no motive—and stressed reasonable doubt. Cunha followed on Friday. Cockran had called him Fickert's "interesting young assistant," but Cunha said, "I have no ill-feeling toward the gentleman who came here from New York to defend this man…He is going back to New York. He is not concerned about San Francisco so much. He is not concerned whether the 'blasters of San Francisco' are at work, and whether we cannot let our mothers and sisters go upon our main streets to watch a parade in safety." The inconsistencies between the testimony of McDonald, who never said anything about a jitney, and that of Oxman, whose testimony implicated Weinberg as well as Billings and the Mooneys, were trifling, said Cunha. Cockran followed again. He reminded the jurors that Bunner had been at Market and Steuart Streets at the same time Oxman said he was but never said anything about a jitney.

Griffin gave final instructions to the jury at about 3:00 p.m. on Friday the ninth. Cockran, certain of acquittal, left to give a lecture. At about 9:30 p.m., the bailiff announced that the jury had reached a verdict. Griffin was sent for. The jury returned, Tom Mooney came in just after. His mother,

Mary; sister, Anna; and Rena's sister, Belle Hammerberg, were already in the room.

MacNevin arose. "We, the members of the jury, find the defendant Thomas J. Mooney guilty of murder in the first degree." There was no recommendation of sentence: Mooney would hang. The courtroom was quiet for a moment, and then Anna screamed, "Oh, my God—Tom, Tom!" Mary Mooney became hysterical: "My boy, my boy—Oh, my God!" Tom tried to comfort her. Israel Weinberg's wife fainted. Belle became hysterical and tried to accost Fickert but was wrested away and removed. The court erupted, and Griffin ordered it cleared.

MacNevin told the press that the jury never doubted that Mooney was guilty; members deliberated only about the penalty. The alternate juror said that Oxman's testimony was the deciding factor. Other jurors would agree. McDonald's testimony just corroborated Oxman's. Cockran was never so dumbfounded by a verdict in his life. He would leave for New York shortly and would not say if he would be associated with the case further. Fickert was flying high. Claiming that the district attorney's office would prosecute seventy-two more crimes, ranging from dynamiting to murder, committed by the same set of men involved in the July 22 bomb, he said, "San Francisco would be amazed to know the extent of the conspiracy of which the Preparedness Day bomb explosion was incidental. We are merely on the threshold of the prosecution to follow this conviction." That evening at the Palace Hotel, Cunha toasted Fickert as California's next governor and himself as San Francisco's next district attorney.

For several weeks after Mooney's conviction, the defense, regrouping after its stinging defeat, submitted affidavits attacking the testimony of prosecution witnesses in the hopes of getting Mooney a new trial. Many were dead ends, but particularly damaging affidavits against the Edeaus came from William Burgess and Thomas Stout of Oakland, co-workers at the clothing store and tailor shop where Mrs. Edeau had worked for about a week. Both men swore that she had told them she was at Market and Steuart but had said nothing about being at 721 Market. Stout also said that Mrs. Edeau had failed to identify Billings and Mooney in their cells, and Burgess corroborated him. When Stout asked her if she didn't think it was wrong to identify innocent men, she said, "What difference does it make? They are only working men. Besides, there are too many working people in the world anyhow." Burgess said that Mrs. Edeau had always expressed contempt for working people and had told him that she would never allow her daughter to marry a workingman. Stout said that he told Mrs. Edeau he thought she would hang a man for fifty cents. "What difference does it make as long as you get paid for it?" she answered. When Stout read about her testimony, with the addition of the jitney in the Mooney trial, he thought that she had gone far enough. He said that his only interest was to see justice done.

Interesting as the affidavits were, Griffin denied the motion for a new trial, and on Saturday, February 24, 1917, he passed sentence. "Under the law I have no other alternative than to pronounce upon you the death penalty, and the judgment of the court and the sentence of the law in this case is that you, Thomas J. Mooney, be delivered by the Sheriff of the City and County of San Francisco to the warden of the State prison at San Quentin to be by him executed and put to death on the 17th day of May, 1917, in the manner provided by the law of the State of California." It was the first time Griffin had sentenced a man to die, and he was plainly disturbed, even departing from the normal wording "that you be hanged by the neck until dead, and may God have mercy on your soul." Mooney was stoic, and there was no outburst by the women.

The *Bulletin*'s coverage of Mooney's trial and post-trial was more favorable to the defense than other papers. The story of Stout's and Burgess's affidavits ran prominently on the front page and continued on page two. The *Examiner* gave it just three paragraphs inside. *Bulletin* reporters, said Older's biographer Evelyn Wells, doubted the prosecution's case, as the story of Fickert plagiarizing Daniel Webster reflected. Older's feelings are hard to define. He had no use for Fickert, whose candidacy for district attorney was a dodge by graft prosecution defendants, but he also had none for Mooney, whom he thought had discredited labor and reform, and believed him guilty. Violence spoiled the world's chances for peace, so why did the oddities in the prosecution's case matter? When McNutt told him that Mooney was innocent, Older told McNutt that he was mistaken. A criminal lawyer told Older that he was suspicious of Oxman. An honest witness skips a beat, has failures of memory. Oxman's testimony sounded too rehearsed. Older was adamant. The editor who was opposed to capital punishment, had, in Wells's words, "stepped out of character and forsaken ideals."

"Let the son of a bitch hang!" Older said.

The Oxman Letters

In the weeks following Mooney's conviction and sentencing, the defense had to regroup and prepare for an appeal for Mooney and for the trials of Rena Mooney and Israel Weinberg (Ed Nolan's had not been scheduled). It had been trying to find something on Oxman but had learned only that he seemed what he purported to be: an Oregon cattleman. A woman in Fresno, California, however, told the defense that she had known Oxman in Grayville, Illinois, a small town on the Wabash River, where he was from originally. And a bellboy at the Terminal Hotel, Market Street, where Oxman said he had registered just before he said he saw Mooney, Billings and the others at Steuart Street with the bomb, told McNutt, "Take it from me, this guy Oxman is a framed witness. I don't know anything about this case, but I got a line on Oxman from that man Rigall." McNutt had only vaguely heard of any "Rigall." After the trial, a Mrs. La Posee said that she had seen Oxman several blocks away from Steuart Street just before the bomb exploded. The lead had been a dead end, but it had provoked a response from Fickert that Oxman would be corroborated by a "John Regal."

Organized labor was reluctant to get involved on behalf of Mooney, now considered a violent radical who had discredited labor and deserved hanging for murder, but he had one conspicuous local ally: the San Francisco chapter of the International Association of Machinists. The International's attorney, Frank Mulholland of Toledo, Ohio, had been hired to represent Nolan. Mooney's defense wanted to investigate Oxman's background

Ed Rigall. *From* The Survey, *July 7, 1917.*

but could not afford to send a detective to Grayville. McNutt got in touch with Mulholland, who got in touch with "Big Ed" Nockles of the Chicago Federation of Labor, who sent two investigators. They checked into the local Grayville Hotel, which happened to be owned by Mrs. F.D. Rigall, a late-middle-aged woman. The investigators, apparently without telling Mrs. Rigall whom they represented, were sent by her to her son, Edward Rigall, at the local pool hall that he owned.

Rigall was not of good repute. He used the pool hall for a gambling business on the side, and he had had scrapes with the law. He was unperturbed by the investigators but said that he would talk about Oxman only through his attorney, Claude Ellis, who was also the mayor. That was a surprise to the investigators, as they hadn't mentioned Oxman. They went to Ellis, who said that he knew about the trip Rigall had taken to San Francisco; this surprised the investigators, too. Then Ellis produced either photographs or originals of letters to Rigall, in longhand on stationery of the Hotel Terminal, San Francisco. The first was undated but had been sent in an envelope postmarked December 14, 1916 (spelling original):

> *Mr. Ed Riggall*
> *Grayville, Ill.*
>
> *Dear Ed:*
>
> *Has been a long time since I hurd from you. I have a chance for you to come to San Francisco as a expurt witness in a very important case. You will only hafto answer 3 to 4 questions and I will Post you on them. You will get mileage and all that a witness can draw probly 100 in the clear so if you will come ans me quick in care of this Hotel and I will mange the Balance*

it is all O.K. but I need a witness Let me know if you can come Jan. 3 is the dait set for trile Pleas keep this confidential.

Answer hear
Yours truly
F.C. Oxman

Rigall had no idea what Oxman was talking about; in fact, he thought the letter was from Oxman's son, also named Frank C., a man about Rigall's age with whom Rigall had been friendly. Rigall had never been to California, and thinking that the younger Oxman was in a scrape and needed help, he anticipated a nice all-expenses-paid trip and wired back, "Will come. Wire transportation and expenses." A few days later, he got a second letter on three sheets of Hotel Terminal stationery, dated December 18:

Dear Ed:

Your Telegram Received I will wire you Transportation in Plenty of time also expce money Will route you by Chicago Omaha U.P. Ogeden S.P. San Frisco. I thought you can make this trip and see California and save a little money. As you will be aloued to collect 10¢ Per Mile from the state which will Be about 200 I can get your expence and you will only hafto say you saw me in San Frisco and that will be easey dun. I will try and meet you on the way out and talk it ovr the state of California will pay you but I will attend to the expces The case wont come up until Jan. 3 or 4 1917 so start about 20 off this month.

You know that the silent Road is the one and say nothing to any Body the fewer People no it the Better when arrive Register as Evansville Ind little more mileage.

Yours truly
F.C. Oxman

Will you want to Return by Los Angeles can Route you that way.

Oxman wrote a third letter to Rigall's mother, inviting her to come out with Ed, ending, "Can probly use a Extry witness been a long time I don't see you." Mrs. Rigall declined to answer, but two days later, Rigall got a telegram, written by Oxman and revised by Fickert, saying that the money for his ticket, plus twenty-seven dollars for expenses, had been sent care of the Illinois Central Railroad ticket agent. In San Francisco, Rigall was to go to the Terminal Hotel and ask for Oxman.

Rigall registered at the hotel on January 6 under the pseudonym "L.O. Charles." Meeting Oxman, he was surprised at seeing a late-middle-aged man, the father of the Frank Oxman he had known in Grayville. Fickert and Cunha were also surprised when they met Rigall. Oxman had told them that he had seen an old schoolmate of his on Preparedness Day who would corroborate his story about Weinberg's jitney, but Rigall was thirty-seven, more than twenty years younger than Oxman. Nonetheless Oxman, Fickert, Cunha and Rigall socialized for about three weeks, enjoying dinners at the Palace Hotel, Tait's and the Cliff House and taking auto and boat rides. Fickert, an Olympic Club member, got Rigall a guest card. But from the moment that Oxman had told Rigall that he wanted him to take the witness stand and say that he (Rigall) had seen Oxman on July 22, Rigall was only playing along and enjoying himself. Just before the trial, Rigall told Oxman that it might be all right for Oxman to testify about the jitney, but Rigall said that he was in Niagara Falls on Preparedness Day. Oxman, according to Rigall, said, "Well, you were here as much as I was."

Rigall said that Fickert, Cunha and Bunner had been rehearsing what he would say on the stand. Then, on the evening of Thursday, January 25, Rigall told Cunha that he could not go along any more: "I was never in San Francisco, and I don't know anything about the case." Cunha, according to Rigall, said, "If that is the case, we won't use you." Rigall had spent the $27 in expense money and was reimbursed $150, and on the Saturday after Oxman testified, uncorroborated by anybody, Rigall boarded a train back to Grayville. Before going, he mentioned to Cunha that Oxman had written him some letters. Cunha asked if he had them with him. Rigall said that they were back in Grayville (they weren't; they were in his pocket). When he got home, he wrote to Cunha asking if he should send Oxman's letters to him or to Fickert. Cunha did not answer.

After Mooney was convicted, Rigall told Ellis everything. Ellis locked the Oxman letters in his safe, and they sent a telegram to Cunha:

> *Congratulations on Your Conviction. Think My Evidence Will Get Party New Trial.*

Cunha immediately wired back:

> *Cannot Understand Your Telegram. You Told Me Your Friend (Oxman) Was Thoroughly Truthful and Reliable. We*

> *Have Plenty of Other Witnesses and Conclusive Evidence Supporting His Testimony. Am Astounded at Your Suggestion that You Have Testimony to Help Defendant. It Is Your Duty to Reveal to Me at Once Any and All Facts You Have, Because I Certainly Want This Defendant to Have a New Trial if He Is Entitled to It. Wire Me Collect…Explain in Detail Your Telegram…Any Witness Who Has Testified Falsely…Must Himself Be Prosecuted for Murder…Send Me All Data…I Am Sure You Know Nothing to Get Defendant New Trial, but…Would…Have Governor Change Penalty or Pardon, if I Developed Any Kind of Doubt…Wire Immediately…at Olympic Club, San Francisco.*

Neither Ellis nor Rigall showed any concern about what might become of Mooney or Billings, or about justice generally. They just realized that the letters and Fickert's Olympic Club pass, also now in Ellis's possession, along with testimony about Oxman's attempt to have Rigall lie on the stand, could be a tremendous embarrassment to the prosecution and were worth money—blackmail, in other words. Rigall's wire was a trap to smoke Cunha out and see what kind of leverage Rigall and Ellis had with him. Cunha's reply betrayed his anxiety that Rigall had something really damaging.

Mulholland had expected only that the investigators would find something discreditable about Oxman in Grayville, and when he got their report, he was astounded. Still, Ellis and Rigall wanted $10,000 for the letters, and the International Workers Defense League was practically broke. In San Francisco, McNutt and lawyers Edward McKenzie and Thomas O'Connor, all now representing Weinberg, were told of the letters, and McKenzie left for the East, hoping to arrange a loan. Ellis, meanwhile, took the letters to Chicago to show them to Mulholland. When he returned to Grayville, he got a shock: his office had been raided, the door lock picked and every drawer, locker, file and book opened and searched. The defense knew that Ellis had taken the letters with him. Whoever searched Ellis's office had to have been sent by the prosecution.

Ellis and Rigall wanted $10,000 for the letters, but they agreed to release them in exchange for a promise of payment later to avoid compromising the defense. In Chicago, defense lawyer Edwin McKenzie had the letters photographed, took them to San Francisco and gave them to McNutt. It was also arranged for Ellis and Rigall to come to San Francisco to testify about Oxman's attempt to suborn perjury.

As Griffin had denied Mooney a new trial and sentenced him, under California law a new trial (without Oxman testifying) would be granted only at the request of the district attorney. (Error in the first trial was not a factor, as Griffin had not committed one. Mooney's only other recourse would be to ask the governor for a pardon.) The defense would pressure Fickert and Cunha by publicizing the letters—in the *Bulletin*, that is—but it had to convince Older, who still believed Mooney was guilty. About the second week of April, Older was called on by Andrew Furuseth of the Coast Seaman's Union, who had seen the letters. Furuseth was a saintly figure who had devoted his whole life to bettering seamen's lives, with little or no reward. Older had once asked Furuseth if he would go to jail because of his work on behalf of seamen, and Furuseth said, "I don't know and I don't care. They can't put me in any smaller room than I have always lived in. They can't feed me any plainer food than I have always eaten. They can't make me any lonelier than I have always been." There were few men Older respected as he did Furuseth.

Furuseth showed Older the letters. As with his forgiveness for Ruef after the graft prosecution, Older had an epiphany, realizing—better late than never—that something was rotten in the Billings-Mooney case. To be sure, the degree of just how much Older swung from belief in Mooney's guilt to belief in his innocence can be debated. He may not have been so much converted as galvanized. The *Bulletin* had derided Fickert from the first time he ran for office, but Older had also said that Mooney was the only person wild enough to plant the Preparedness Day bomb, and he had no evidence of impropriety by the prosecution until he saw the Oxman letters.

Older wanted to publish the letters as soon as he had verified their authenticity, but he could not afford to risk having his publisher, Crothers, and Crothers's nephew, Pickering, stop him. To counter their presumed opposition—a presumption that turned out all too accurate—Older presented them with a *fait accompli*. Late on Wednesday April 11, probably after Crothers and Pickering had left for the day, the *Bulletin* ran a "jackrabbit" late-night extra, with two lines across the top half of the front page blaring, "Oxman Framed to Hang Tom Mooney." That extra probably sold out, leaving readers wanting details, and the next day, Thursday the twelfth, the *Bulletin* supplied them. It was just six days after the United States had declared war in Europe, and while the front pages of most American newspapers were mostly war news, the first two pages of the *Bulletin* were devoted almost entirely to the Oxman letters. A page-one headline proclaimed, "Mooney

Plot Exposed." A subhead charged Cunha, Fickert and Bunner with plotting to hang Mooney by perjury. Photographs of the letters, on Hotel Terminal stationery, filled four columns on page two, their authenticity confirmed by handwriting and photography expert Theodore Kytka, with captions saying that Oxman had suborned perjury.

A box on page two, column five, listed charges by Israel Weinberg's lawyer, Thomas O'Connor: "No sane man can doubt that Oxman testified falsely. Every word that he uttered upon the stand…was basely, feloniously and absolutely false." O'Connor's claims were exaggerated. While the Oxman letters were felonious in that they suborned perjury by Rigall, they did not suggest that Oxman himself had lied. But they did raise serious doubts about the prosecution's star witness.

For the rest of the week and most of the next, the *Bulletin* ratcheted up the pressure. Fickert being away on Thursday, Cunha issued a statement claiming that Rigall wanted to testify even after Oxman said that he was not the man he had seen on July 22, but that he, Cunha, "would not stand for it. I believed he was the bunk, and I put no faith in his statements." Cunha caught himself *and* Oxman in a web of contradictions. During cross-examination by Cockran, Oxman had maintained that in his ranching business, he had cultivated an acute memory for faces and was able to identify people a year after having seeing them only once, but he had referred to Rigall as both a "young man," as Cunha said, and "old schoolmate," which would have made Rigall anywhere between twenty and sixty. Worse for Cunha, four newspapers had quoted the prosecution on February 14 that it would call "John Rigall, an Oregon businessman," to corroborate Oxman's testimony, almost three weeks after Cunha said that he would not stand for Rigall's testimony and after Rigall told Cunha that he wasn't in San Francisco and knew nothing about the case.

Fickert returned to San Francisco on Friday, April 13. He dismissed the *Bulletin*'s charges as "nothing new in criminal practice…and particularly in bomb-throwing cases." He would continue to prosecute all the defendants and would call Oxman as a witness again. The newspapers reported that Oxman was coming to San Francisco from Oregon, and Rigall was on his way from Illinois.

But while Fickert professed to be confident that Oxman's testimony would hold up and that he would call him again, Saturday's *Bulletin* exposed very discreditable information about Oxman's history. On the front page, competing for reader's attention about war news, was the headline, "Suits in East Reveal Oxman Deals in Land." The story began with a telegram from the *Princeton*

Democrat of Princeton, Indiana, relating that Oxman had been indicted by a grand jury on a charge of false pretense. On page two, just three columns to the right of the article about Fickert—the placement was probably deliberate—the story continued. Oxman and his brother, Clarence, according to the *Democrat*, had showed Meyer Green a desirable piece of grazing land, with livestock, that Oxman did not own. When Green learned that the land he had really bought from Oxman was a swamp, he sued and was awarded $4,000. Oxman had pulled a similar deal with a man named Pratt whom the *Democrat* noted "was manipulated with Oxman's usual misrepresentations."

It would come out later that Oxman had married a Grayville woman in 1880 but deserted her in 1900 to go to Oregon with a young unmarried girl. They parted, but in 1904, Oxman married another woman without being divorced from his first wife. He married the second woman again in 1911 when the divorce was granted. An even stranger story would come out about an Oregon trial. A man named Spain had sued the Oregon-Washington Railroad and Navigation Company, claiming that the railroad had unlawfully ejected him from a train. Oxman offered to testify that Spain was drunk and disorderly, justifying the ejection, and said that his testimony would be corroborated by a man named Regal, whom he said worked for him. Before taking Oxman up on his offer of "help," a railroad agent investigated and found that there was no "Regal" in that part of Oregon. Why Oxman sought out Rigall in either trial was never explained, nor was it clear why and how he turned up as a witness against Mooney.

When a big story broke, Older often stayed in San Francisco rather than going home to Cupertino. When he was at the Fairmont Hotel on Friday evening, Cunha knocked on the door. He was in great distress over the Oxman letters: "Well, I guess I'm in the ash-can." Cunha said that he had believed that Mooney and Billings were guilty, but he did not want to convict them on perjured testimony. On the morning of Saturday the fourteenth, Cunha, Older and defense attorneys Thomas O'Connor and Edwin McKenzie met in Older's office. Cunha, said Older, definitely agreed to a new trial for Mooney. O'Connor and McKenzie corroborated Older. O'Connor and Cunha met that afternoon in O'Connor's office, and "it was definitely agreed that Fickert and Cunha were to immediately request the Attorney General to confess error in the trial of Mooney," according to O'Connor. The Supreme Court would grant a new trial, and if Mooney were acquitted, which Cunha considered inevitable, Fickert's office would confess to error in Billings's case, and all of the defendants in the bomb cases were to be dismissed.

On Sunday, McKenzie, O'Connor and Cunha were to go to Older's property above Cupertino to discuss the agreement. O'Connor and McKenzie drove in O'Connor's car to the Olympic Club on Post Street, where Cunha had a room. As they were all in the car, a *Chronicle* reporter came along and spoke to O'Connor. Cunha was suddenly concerned that being seen with defense attorneys might be unwise and got out of the car. He said that he wasn't needed anyway, and O'Connor and McKenzie went without him.

On Monday, there was another meeting of Cunha, the defense attorneys and Older. Cunha said that he was ready to stand by the agreement for the defendants' release, but he was distressed: "I know I'm in the dump heap for the rest of my life, but if you think you're going to get me in jail you're mistaken." Older said, "Cunha, I don't want to 'get' anybody. My position is just this: Here is the evidence that these men were the victims of a perjury conspiracy. All I want is to see that they get a square deal."

That afternoon, Captain Duncan Matheson and former sergeant (now lieutenant) Charles Goff called on Older. The Oxman letters had precipitated, or at least coincided with, a final break between Matheson and the district attorney's office. Matheson had been quoted in the newspapers that the case was a "nasty mess" and said that he wanted to conduct his own investigation of Oxman independent of Fickert. Older, Goff and Matheson discussed the discrepancies between Oxman's and McDonald's testimony. Matheson drew a diagram of Market and Steuart Streets, and Older pointed out that McDonald had testified that Billings and Mooney had walked north across Market Street after supposedly depositing the suitcase, but Oxman said that they got back in the car and drove south down Steuart. Goff said that they might have gone through the procession and then back to the car—he didn't suggest *why* they would have done that—but Older said, "You're eating up time pretty fast. You must remember that McDonald testified that the suitcase was planted at eight or ten minutes to two. You must get Mooney up on the Eilers building by one and a half minutes after two because he showed up in a photograph at that time."

Matheson looked at Goff and said, "Charlie, this won't do. There is something wrong." Goff agreed.

On Wednesday, April 18, Ed Rigall arrived in San Francisco along with his wife, mother and attorney, Claude Ellis. Oxman arrived later the same day. Rigall stated publicly that Fickert and Cunha had connived with

Oxman to get him, Rigall, to corroborate Oxman's testimony, without even knowing if Rigall was in San Francisco on Preparedness Day. On the basis of a complaint by defense attorney McKenzie, police court justice Matthew Brady issued a warrant for Oxman's arrest for subornation of perjury. Oxman told Captain Matheson, "I would say that I have been given a rough and scurvy deal, and that the people of San Francisco ought to know it. I came here voluntarily to give my testimony, and the first thing I find is that the District Attorney's office and the police department have turned against me. I don't think that's right or fair." Matheson replied that all he wanted was the truth. Oxman was booked, and after posting $2,000 cash bail, he went to the office of attorney Samuel Shortridge. He protested that this was the first time in his life that he had a warrant served against him, which, as the *Bulletin* had printed earlier, was not true.

On the night of the same Wednesday the eighteenth, there was another meeting at the Olympic Club between Older, defense attorneys McKenzie and O'Connor, Cunha, Fickert and Fickert's attorney, Harry Stafford. Fickert said that all he wanted was a statement from Oxman absolving the district attorney's office of blame; after that, he would set the machinery in motion to get Mooney a new trial. It was agreed that the grand jury would stay out of the affair, that the remaining cases would depend for their dismissal on the result of Mooney's second trial and that a statement would be given to the newspapers to that effect. Fickert shook hands warmly with everyone and left. Cunha said that he would go to the district attorney's office to prepare the newspaper statement. Before leaving, he shook hands with Fremont Older, and with tears in his eyes, he said, "You are a great, big, fine fellow; you are the biggest man in San Francisco and you are doing a generous, kindly and decent act for us."

In less than two days, the agreement collapsed. On Wednesday night, Fickert, contrary to what he had promised, appeared before the grand jury in a midnight session and asked that he alone be allowed to investigate Oxman, which would put him in the position of investigating his own witness who was suspected of perjury. Fickert had also put Oxman in touch with attorney Shortridge, who was grand jury foreman John Spreckels's lawyer. The grand jury was under Fickert's control, but it denied Fickert's request and asked state attorney general Ulysses Webb to appoint a special investigator. On Friday morning, Fickert said that he would ask a new trial for Mooney only if Oxman's testimony were proven false but that nothing had convinced him that it was. Fickert followed that by charging in the *Examiner* that Older had entertained the anarchist Emma Goldman at his property and somehow had guilty foreknowledge of the Preparedness Day bomb:

> *I don't mind saying that Mr. Older himself may yet have to answer questions as a witness in the trials growing out of the bomb plot cases. The Grand Jury would also be justified in calling him as a witness in inquiring into some of the occurrences prior to Preparedness Day, for Older knows more about them than he has ever published in his newspaper.*

Older read Fickert's fantastic charge in Friday morning's *Examiner*, and that afternoon, the *Bulletin* printed Older's account of the meetings of the previous week, with corroboration by O'Connor and McKenzie. Older said that if Fickert really had information linking him with the bomb, Fickert should have presented it nine months earlier after the bomb exploded instead of waiting until after the *Bulletin* printed the Oxman letters. Fickert had announced that he would subpoena Older to testify before the grand jury, but no subpoena was issued, and on Friday evening, Older called Fickert's bluff by going to the grand jury chambers and waiting conspicuously for an hour and a half by the door, where Fickert and others saw him. When Older was still not called, he printed an open letter in the *Bulletin* to grand jury foreman Spreckels saying that he, Older, would appear at the grand jury session on Wednesday the twenty-fifth for a hearing: "In the event of its being granted I shall reserve the right to give as wide publicity to the result of the proceedings as Fickert gave to the accusation."

On Tuesday, April 24, the *Examiner* printed a lengthy article by Fickert in which he charged that

> [a]*n adroit and heavily financed campaign is being made to convince you…that Billings and Mooney…have been made the victims of an infamous conspiracy.* [There was a] *formulated policy of these bloodthirsty anarchists to escape punishment for their crimes…Its exemplification is found in the Bulletin every day, and Mr. Older of the Bulletin has been an adviser of these murderers, even to assisting them in the selection of counsel.*

On the evening of Wednesday the twenty-fifth, Older, accompanied by three defense attorneys, went to Foreman Spreckels and demanded to be heard on Fickert's charge. Spreckels said that he hadn't heard of any charge and summoned Fickert from the next room. Fickert said that he would conduct the hearing when he was ready and led Older out by the arm: "You get out of this room! You have no business in here, and neither have these men with you." After Older and the attorneys had been waiting in an anteroom, a committee of three grand jurors said that he would be called to Attorney General Webb's investigation of Oxman.

Webb designated former Superior Court judge Robert M. Clarke to conduct the investigation. Clarke granted Older's hearing, although he said that it had no bearing on the investigation. Several jurors questioned Older informally, but the questioning produced nothing new until Older was asked if a purported feud between himself and Fickert had anything to do with the *Bulletin* exposé. "No," said Older, "I have no feeling against any human being." "Do you mean you have no feeling against Oxman?" another juror asked. Older answered. "No. How could I have any feeling against an insane man? Nobody but an insane man would do anything like that."

On May 3, after a fourteen-to-three vote, the grand jury announced that "after a careful and conscientious investigation we find no cause for criticism of the District Attorney's office in connection with the bomb cases," and it unanimously commended Fickert for his "able and fearless manner." The next day, Judge Clarke disagreed, saying that the evidence justified indicting Oxman. Judge Matthew Brady agreed and had Oxman bound over for trial.

Fickert's abrupt turnaround from the agreement reached on the weekend may been due to outside influence. He was in regular contact with the chamber of commerce and the Law and Order Committee, both of which were more interested in following up with their victory over organized labor than in strict pursuit of justice. The agreement between Fickert and Older, corroborated by O'Connor and McKenzie, may have been just a delaying tactic until the businessmen's groups decided what to do.

Another rationale for continuing to prosecute the original defendants appeared in *The Survey* magazine for July 7, 1917. On June 14, *Survey* staffer John A. Fitch interviewed Cunha in his office. Fitch asked Cunha if he might clarify some facts about Oxman, but instead of replying to the question, Cunha erupted:

> *If the thing were done that ought to be done the whole dirty low-down bunch would be taken out and strung up without ceremony.*
>
> *They're a bunch of dirty anarchists. They're a bunch of dirty anarchists, every one of them, and they ought to be in jail on general principles. I'm disgusted with all this outcry over Mooney—making a hero of him, when he's an anarchist and a murderer. If he ought to be out of jail, let him get*

> *out. The courts are open to him. But I'm not going to help. If I knew that every single witness that testified against him had perjured himself in his testimony I wouldn't lift a finger to get him a new trial.*
>
> *And now people like Judge Griffin are going around saying he ought to have a new trial. Judge Griffin almost cried there on the bench because we searched the* Blast *office without a warrant…*
>
> *Do you think I was going to wait around two or three days for a search warrant for people like that? Now if it was your house or mine it would be different, but I'm glad there was a district attorney's office here with guts enough to go ahead and search those people without waiting for a warrant.*
>
> *And they let such people talk on the streets! If I had my way I'd get a bunch of cops and go after them and beat their heads off.*

Fitch was hardly able to get a word in, but he finally asked Cunha if he didn't think it was wrong for law officers to act in defiance of the law. Not when somebody like Berkman or Mooney was involved, replied Cunha. When Fitch observed that being an anarchist was not illegal, Cunha snapped back, "I consider that it is."

"It isn't a question of what you consider it to be," put in Fitch. "You know as a matter of fact that the law defines no such crime." Finally getting around to the subject of Oxman, Cunha said that there was enough evidence to convict Mooney without Oxman's testimony.

As the tumultuous month of April ended, Fickert announced that he would proceed to prosecute Rena Mooney and Israel Weinberg. Ed Nolan, however, was released on bail after Assistant District Attorney Louis Ferrari said that there was insufficient evidence to hold him; Duncan Matheson said that he had been opposed to Nolan's arrest from the very beginning. Matheson also said that Estelle Smith told him that Oxman had offered her "a sum in five figures" if she would testify that she had seen Weinberg at 721 Market Street. She said that she told Oxman she never saw Weinberg in her life.

Most significantly, Judge Griffin wrote to Attorney General Webb asking that Mooney's case be returned to his, Griffin's, jurisdiction because of the Oxman letters:

> *In the trial of Mooney, there was called as a witness by the People one Frank C. Oxman, whose testimony was most damaging and of the utmost consequence…Indeed, in my opinion, the testimony of this witness was by far the most important adduced by the People…*

> *Within the past week there have been brought to my attention certain letters written by Oxman…The authorship and authenticity of these letters…are undenied and undisputed. As you will see, they bear directly upon the credibility of the witness and go to the very foundation of the truth of the story told by Oxman on the witness stand. Had they been before me at the time of the hearing of the motion for new trial, I would unhesitatingly have granted it…*
>
> *In the circumstances of this case, I believe that all of us who were participants in the trial concur that right and justice demand that new trial of Mooney should be had in order that no possible mistake shall be made in a case where a human life is at stake.*

Judge Dunne, in whose court Billings had been convicted and who was scheduled to preside at Rena Mooney's trial, took a very different view. Billings's statement about his whereabouts on Preparedness Day, said Dunne, "was perjury so plain and palpable that it would not have deceived a jury of children." He added that "poison gas" was being "spread…to obstruct and injure the administration of justice," with the help of "every crooked, cowardly, blackguard lawyer who is going around the community with a letter of marque in the shape of a license to practice."

Fickert was coming under fire in newspapers all over the state, and in Sacramento, there were rumors of a recall election. One John Stephens of San Francisco wrote to Fremont Older:

> *I haven't any time for this fellow Mooney, who in my judgment has done… the cause of labor more harm than good; while, as for Hearst, if he was dying of thirst and I had the only bucket of water in the world I would moisten a rose bush with it. But…this case shows us that there is something in the office of the District Attorney so rotten it threatens to spread contagion. If this fellow Fickert can railroad Mooney to the scaffold, who among us is safe? I always understood it was the duty of the District Attorney to protect, not only the State and its interests, but the defense and its interests, and that, when he saw a doubt of the guilt of the accused, to give him the benefit. But it appears that this person is willing to use perjured testimony and protect the perjurer.*
>
> *Keep up the fight, Mr. Older; the citizens are behind you.*

Billings-Mooney Becomes International

On Monday, April 23, there was a radical new development in the Billings-Mooney case. On Wednesday the twenty-fifth, the *New York Times* reported from Petrograd (St. Petersburg) that on Monday, a "small group of ultra-radicals" led by "Nikolai Lenine" had tried to make an "unfriendly demonstration" before the American embassy. The purported leader, who was not actually present, was Vladimir Ilyich Ulyanov, better known as "Lenin," which American newspapers misspelled. Militiamen turned back the demonstrators on the Nevsky Prospect, but American ambassador Charles Francis heard chanting about something like "Muni." Francis had no idea who "Muni" was and cabled the American secretary of state for information. The *Times* noted that the person referred to "probably is Thomas J. Mooney, who is under sentence of death for connection with the bomb explosion in San Francisco in July 1916, in which several persons were killed."

Just three weeks earlier, the United States had declared war on the Central Powers, and the European "Great War" was now what would be called World War I. In Russia, Tsar Nicholas II had abdicated. Kerensky's provisional government had taken power and was continuing Russian participation in the war, tying down a great part of Germany's army. President Wilson's administration needed good relations with Russia, as well as American labor's cooperation. Hiram Johnson had been elected United States senator from California in 1916 and was succeeded by Lieutenant Governor William Stephens. President Wilson, who may have seen the Oxman letters after the *Bulletin* printed them, telegrammed Stephens:

ANTI-AMERICAN OUTBURST

Extremists Attempt to Demonstrate at Embassy Because of Supposed Hanging of Mooney.

Special Cable to THE NEW YORK TIMES.
PETROGRAD, April 24. (Dispatch to

New York Times headline, April 25, 1917.

> *I hope that in view of certain international aspects which the case has assumed you will not deem me impertinent or beyond my rights if I very warmly and earnestly urge upon you the wisdom and desirability of commuting the sentence of Mooney or at least suspending its execution until the charges of perjury lodged against the witnesses in the case are judicially probed to the bottom. Such an action on your part would, I can assure you, have the widest and most beneficial results and greatly relieve some critical situations outside the United States.*

Governor Stephens replied that as Mooney's case was being appealed, his execution was already suspended, and Wilson wrote back that he was relieved. But demonstrations like that in Petrograd were spreading. In Holland, on May 11, the National Laborers Organization, representing numerous craft unions, sent a message signed by twenty labor chairmen and secretaries to the American ambassador in The Hague:

> *Excellency: The undersigned…having heard of the ignominious trial now in progress, by the aid of intriguing and corrupt officials…in San Francisco, in which…Thomas J. Mooney and his wife, Warren K.*

> *Billings and Israel Weinberg, are on trial, and having heard that this case has brought one of these leaders to the point of judicial murder...* [we] *are resolved to protest with all their force against such an infamous outcome of American "justice."*
>
> *The hope for the honor of the...United States, which claims to have taken part in the world war in behalf of democracy...forbids that sons of their own country shall be murdered or condemned to martyrdom in jail—men whose crime was nothing else than that they were fighters...for the freedom of the wage slaves.*

In Chicago, E.N. Nockles, secretary of the 400,000-member Chicago Federation of Labor, sent a telegram to California's Governor Stephens and Attorney General Webb:

> *Is it not rather astounding in face of documentary and undisputable evidence...that District Attorney Fickert of San Francisco is still at large, permitted to hold public office, permitted to prosecute or persecute against those he framed...Should he not at least be removed from office pending an investigation of his illegal acts? Or does it make a difference to the great State of California whose ox is gored?*

This was only the beginning. The Billings-Mooney case was no longer a local matter; it was national and international. San Francisco was becoming polarized. Prosecution supporters fired back. The *Argonaut* magazine for May 5, 1917, ran an editorial under the head, "Back-Fire in the Bomb Cases," disparaging the whole issue of Oxman's testimony and the letters:

> *The expedient known as "back-fire" is one of the commonest means of evading or defeating whatever may appear in the shape of an impending menace. We have just now in San Francisco a significant application of this device in connection with the bomb cases. Two men whose guilt is both a moral and a legal assurance are under conviction as active agents in the setting-off of an infernal machine* [during]*...the great Preparedness parade...*
>
> *Ordinary—even extraordinary—means of defense having failed, there is now recourse to the device of back-fire. The effort is to divert attention from the main issue, namely, the innocence or guilt of the convicted or indicted defendants...Among other things an attempt has been made to break down the character of a witness, one Oxman, and farmer and cattleman of Oregon, who gave positive testimony in the trial of Mooney. While the*

> *evidence of Oxman was not essential to the case of the prosecution it had definite value as sustaining and assuring the testimony of other witnesses…*
>
> *Thus concurrently we see intruded into the matter an issue of privilege raised by the familiar and unsavory figure of Fremont Older. In all this there is an obvious purpose to elevate non-essentials and to subordinate essentials—to discredit the prosecution and to break down the machinery of justice.*

On Tuesday, April 24, Fickert publicly appealed for support. On Saturday, April 28, the Law and Order Committee placed a full-page advertisement, headlined, "Law and Order—To the Men and Women of San Francisco," in every major newspaper except the *Bulletin*. After reminding the city of the meeting in Civic Auditorium just after Preparedness Day, the committee claimed that while San Francisco's citizens were devoting time and energy to the war effort:

> [T]*hose very forces that made the bomb outrage of Preparedness day possible have been taking Full and Measured and Unscrupulous Advantage of you to spread their doctrine of anarchy, their intimidation of courts and of elected officials.*
>
> *Coercion of courts, peremptory demands on elected officials that the Law be arbitrarily set aside are a far more devilish expression of anarchy than was the bomb outrage itself.*

The very next Monday, there was another advertisement headlined, "Law and Order—To the Men and Women of San Francisco." The advertisement was sign by a committee of citizens, including several labor leaders, former mayor P.H. McCarthy, two state senators and the Speaker pro tem of the California Assembly. At first glance, it looked like Saturday's ad and began, "As men and women and as citizens, we affirm our belief in Law and Order." The threat to "Law and Order" referred to in Monday's ad, however, was from the district attorney's office, which had put Oxman on the witness stand knowing that he had tried to get Rigall to commit perjury. As for the Law and Order Committee's charge that criticism of the district attorney was "anarchy" perpetrated by "those very forces that made the bomb outrage of Preparedness day possible," Monday's ad read, "Certainly the insistence upon the faithful enforcement of the law in the exposure and punishment of perjury is not a defense of anarchy, and such insistence does not brand those who take this stand as the instigators of the Preparedness Day crime."

Fickert had said that he would begin Rena Mooney's murder trial on Monday, April 23, 1917, but he was not ready until Monday, May 21. The case was assigned to Judge Dunne's court. Because of what Dunne had said in April about Billings and the defense lawyers, the defense charged that he was prejudiced. He denied it but said that he would not preside in any of the remaining cases and called in Superior Judge Emmet Seawell of Santa Rosa. Contributions had poured in for the defense after the Oxman letters, and Rena was represented by McNutt, McKenzie, O'Connor, Charles Brennan and Nathan Coghlan. Assistant District Attorney Louis Ferrari prosecuted, with assistance from lawyer Charles Cobb, whom the Law and Order Committee had sponsored. Cobb had been the law partner of Francis Heney of the graft prosecution and was the last person Fremont Older had spoken to before Older was kidnapped in September 1907. His participation was one more sign of the split in the old graft prosecution over Billings and Mooney.

Jury selection took three weeks. Ferrari made the first argument for the prosecution on Monday, June 11. He alleged a conspiracy of which Rena was "Lady Macbeth," but he obviously had a weak case. The only evidence he cited against Rena was that she bought niter, used in making dynamite, and that she was connected with radical politics. When he finished, McNutt asked the court's permission to ask the prosecution a question: would Ferrari give the probable date when F.C. Oxman would be put on the witness stand? The defense wished to bring witnesses from the East and from Oregon and did not wish to be taken by surprise. Ferrari said that he would give the defense ample notice if Oxman were to be called.

Oxman was not called as a witness at Rena's or any other trial. The prosecution called Estelle Smith, McDonald, the Edeaus and Samuel Samuels, a longshoreman who said that he sold Rena niter just before Preparedness Day. Estelle Smith had not been a witness at Tom Mooney's trial, probably because of the newspaper stories about her background, which seemed to have affected her composure. She accused Tom's mother, Mary, of making faces at her—Mary had a facial tic—and she changed her testimony again from what she had told the grand jury. McDonald also changed his testimony from Mooney's trial, which the defense said was obviously done to have his story corroborate Estelle Smith's latest one. The defense produced two Salvation Army men who said that McDonald bragged about the money he was getting to testify and who added that he had an untruthful reputation. Sadie Edeau dropped a bombshell by saying she had given Fickert a statement identifying the defendants before she had seen them.

McKenzie asked, "At the time you made this statement you had not seen these defendants in jail?"

"No."

"How could you identify them, then?"

"There was something else put on my statement after lunch."

"But you signed it, didn't you?"

"If it was legally signed, I signed it."

Sadie Edeau seemed so confused that Judge Seawell asked her how she happened to mention the defendants by name. "I didn't think I did. My mother had told me about them."

Samuel Samuels completely discredited his testimony about selling Rena niter when he said that he had never discussed the case with his brother, a police officer. Ferrari had visited Samuels accompanied by Samuels's brother, whom Samuels didn't recognize. Defense lawyer O'Connor called Samuels "the Oxman of the Rena Mooney case."

Sunday, July 22, was the first anniversary of Preparedness Day. The jury, which Judge Seawell had ordered locked up daily, retired late in the morning of Tuesday, July 24, after the longest trial since the graft prosecution. It deliberated over two days and twice reported that it was hopelessly deadlocked; shouting and name-calling were heard from the jury room. Finally, after more than fifty hours, the jurors returned a verdict: not guilty. But Rena was not free. The grand jury had returned eight indictments against her, and Fickert said that he would try her on each of them. He attributed her acquittal to a male jury's reluctance to convict a woman, and as women in California could now be jurors, he planned to get as many women as possible on the next jury. Judge Dunne, a member of the three-judge panel that granted bail, refused it. The Mooneys, Billings and Weinberg began their second year in jail.

On Monday, July 30, the defense got what looked like a victory when state attorney general Ulysses Webb agreed to Judge Griffin's request and filed a formal consent to a reversal of the judgment against Tom Mooney. The *Bulletin* reported that it was "tantamount to the issuance by the Supreme Court of an order for a new trial," but unfortunately it wasn't. In September, the Supreme Court denied Webb's request: once ten days had passed after sentencing, said the court, it could not consider new evidence that did not appear in the trial record; the Oxman letters did not appear until two months after sentencing. Fickert's office had argued that the court could grant a new trial only if reversible errors in the trial were found, and none were. The Supreme Court, however, was still considering Mooney's appeal, which would be heard in March 1918. If that failed, Mooney would have to appeal to the governor.

Late in October 1917, fifteen months after Preparedness Day, Israel Weinberg went on trial. The *Bulletin* called it a pathetic spectacle:

> *Mr. Ferrari will try to prove that Billings, Mr. and Mrs. Mooney and Weinberg were in front of 721 Market Street at 1:30 on the day of the explosion. The only witnesses to this effect are Mrs. Edeau and her daughter, who originally offered to testify that they saw the defendants at Steuart and Market streets, and whose testimony before a jury with the least rudiments of intelligence is worse than valueless. The testimony placing Billings at 721 Market Street has already been shaken by equally reliable—or unreliable, as the case may be—testimony placing him in two other spots… And the rest of Weinberg's imaginary pilgrimage to the scene of the bomb outrage is quite as shaky. Police Sergeant Goff, who was on duty on Market Street at the time of the explosion, has stated that Weinberg's automobile did not come down Market Street below Third during the time required by the prosecution's theory…The truth is that Weinberg had no more to do with the bomb explosion than any other man picked at random out of a crowd of five hundred thousand people. The only offenses he ever committed were to send his little boy to study music under Mrs. Mooney and to drive Mr. and Mrs. Mooney home from a meeting at which the heinous sin of creating a strike on the United Railroads was discussed.*

At trial, Ferrari produced articles from the *Blast*, suggesting that if Weinberg read it, he must have had something to do with the bombing. He called neither Estelle Smith nor Oxman, only McDonald and Mrs. Edeau, who said that she saw Weinberg and his jitney at 721 Market. On Monday, November 12, as the trial was in progress, the *Bulletin* revealed one of the most bizarre episodes to date in the Billings-Mooney cases. On January 29, 1917, the Edeaus testified seeing the Mooneys, Billings and a man in a vehicle at 721 Market Street. On the thirtieth, Fickert called Oakland police inspector William Smith to his office and told him that he wanted him to corroborate the Edeaus' testimony. Smith refused. The Oakland Police Department required its officers to keep diaries. Smith recorded his movements on index cards and showed Fickert the one for July 28, 1916, when he had accompanied Mrs. Edeau to San Francisco when Sergeant Goff asked her to identify Billings and Mooney in their cells:

> *Took Mrs. Edeau of 4106 Bayo St. to S.F. to see if she could identify Tom Mooney and Warren K. Billings as men she saw with suit case at Market and Steuart St.*
>
> *She failed to identify them.*

Fickert said, "Smith, you'd make a damned good witness for the defense. Keep your mouth shut about this thing."

As Mrs. Edeau had originally told Smith, she and Sadie were at Market and Steuart Streets. Oakland police chief Walter Peterson was surprised to read that she testified being more than four thousand feet southwest at 721 Market—her testimony put the Edeaus in two places at once. On Thursday, April 12, 1917, the day the *Bulletin* printed the Oxman letters, Older, Smith and defense attorneys Charles Brennan (not to be confused with Billings's prosecutor, James Brennan), McKenzie and O'Connor went to question Mrs. Edeau about the discrepancies between what she and daughter, Sadie, had told Smith and what they said in court. Mrs. Edeau, alone in her home in the Oakland hills near Mills College, seemed distressed. Older apparently sent for Chief Peterson to reassure her. In the front room, Mrs. Edeau rambled about the brown eyes of her dead husband looking down at her, but she corroborated Smith's account that she had told him only that she was at Steuart Street and had not identified Billings or Mooney in their cells. Pressed as to why she had changed her story, she said, "I did not want to tell all I knew. I would not tell Smith they were the men. But in my heart I was sure they were the men. Something in my soul kept telling me."

As Older, Smith, Brennan and McKenzie were just outside on the porch and O'Connor and Mrs. Edeau were in the front room, Mrs. Edeau suddenly became hysterical. Opening a table drawer and saying that she would have protection, she took out a revolver. O'Connor caught her by the wrist, took the gun away and handed it to Smith, who shook out the cartridges. When Peterson arrived, Mrs. Edeau calmed down, and the interview continued. The men asked her about being at Steuart Street and 721 Market at the same time. Her answer became part of the rapidly growing Billings-Mooney folklore: her physical body, said Mrs. Edeau, was at Steuart Street, but her astral self was at 721 Market. She saw Billings, the Mooneys and the car with her astral eyes.

At trial, O'Connor said that although it was difficult to understand many things in this case, Mrs. Edeau solved everything: "Her astral body was at 721 Market Street. And thus…she saw an astral suitcase, and an astral Weinberg, driving an astral jitney, and that, of course, accounts for

The Edeaus: daughter Sadie (standing) and mother Mellie, who claimed that her physical body was at Steuart Street while her astral self saw Billings at 721 Market almost a mile west. *Bancroft Library*.

its going down Market Street in the face of the parade, past the twenty or thirty thousand marchers, and all the policemen and all the bystanders, and was seen only by Mrs. Edeau. And the reason for that is simple, gentlemen, when you know that it was the astral Weinberg who drove the astral Ford."

On Tuesday, November 27, the jury retired just long enough to look up "astral" in the encyclopedia, and without deliberating, it returned in twenty-five minutes with a verdict: not guilty. It was, said the *Bulletin*, the quickest verdict in a major case in San Francisco's history. "I think we all had pretty definite ideas about the credibility of this particular astral body which wandered up Market Street and spotted Weinberg," said one juror. "I'm not a lawyer, but this is the first I ever heard of an astral identification of a man on trial for his life." Another juror was more emphatic:

> *Wine bums and bats! Can anyone who heard John McDonald and the Edeau woman testify suppose for a moment that any jury having the sense that God gave geese would believe them for half a minute? That woman didn't dare look at us when she said she had seen Weinberg. She was looking toward Pine Street and she didn't raise her eyes. And then there was her astral body!*
>
> *I own property and I believe in the law and I'm against anarchists; and I went into this case with an absolutely open mind, and I was ready to convict on any kind of adequate showing of evidence—but not on a wild-eyed, astral-bodied, wine-bum case like that!*

Assistant DA Ferrari had said that "Weinberg and the other defendants must stand or fall together." The jury's emphatic dismissal of the prosecution's case seemed to overthrow the cases against all defendants, Billings and Mooney included. Optimistically, the *Bulletin* noted, "This is the beginning of the end of this frame-up." Unfortunately, it wasn't. Weinberg's acquittal did not end his troubles any more than Rena Mooney's acquittal ended hers. Fickert said that he would try him on the remaining indictments, and Judge Dunne still resisted granting bail. Older was losing patience with his old ally, Judge Dunne, and the *Bulletin* kept up the attack on Fickert:

> *The malice and stupidity of District Attorney Fickert kept Israel Weinberg sixteen months in jail, ruined his business, swept away the savings of a lifetime, and reduced his wife and children to want. It took the jury in Weinberg's case just* [twenty-five] *minutes to topple the whole mass of perjury and fraud and expose the prosecution—or persecution—for the miserable conspiracy it actually was…*
>
> *There is not even a remote possibility of convicting either prisoner at a further trial. No one knows this better than Fickert or better than Judge Dunne, who is directly responsible for keeping Mrs. Mooney and Weinberg in jail…An unprejudiced judge would release both, on reasonable bail, without question…Judge Dunne is a spectacle for cynics—once a fearless foe of the system and interests represented by Fickert, now…playing directly into its hands; an honest man doing a dishonest man's work.*

Oxman finally went on trial for subornation of perjury in September 1917, in Dunne's court. Attorney General Webb appointed Deputy Attorney

General Raymond Benjamin as special prosecutor the day before the trial began. As Dunne had said publicly that there was nothing incriminating in the Oxman letters, as well as was hostile to the Mooney defense, and as Benjamin was an unenthusiastic prosecutor and a friend of Fickert's, acquittal was inevitable. Benjamin's only major witness was Rigall, whose unsavory past was laid out by Oxman's attorney, Shortridge. Oxman was acquitted on September 28 but was rearrested on a warrant signed by Judge Griffin on the basis of a complaint by Mooney's attorneys charging Oxman with perjury. The attorneys alleged that Oxman had not even been in San Francisco when the bomb went off but rather was in Woodland, California, ninety miles away. They said that there was a witness, unnamed, but were unable to produce him, and on October 4, Griffin dismissed the perjury charge. Oxman went back to Oregon and lived in seclusion. Why he told his preposterous story in Mooney's trial and how Fickert found him were never fully explained.

A movement to recall Fickert had begun in April just after the Oxman letters appeared. Fickert tried every kind of legal and extralegal tactic to stop it, but an election was finally set for Tuesday, December 18, 1917. Unfortunately for the recall movement, Fickert had two opponents: former police commissioner Charles Sweigert and lawyer Frank P. Haynes. Sweigert campaigned on the Billings-Mooney scandal and on Fickert's non-enforcement of laws against prostitution. He was endorsed by numerous clergymen, the *Bulletin*, Rudolph Spreckels, Furuseth and other labor leaders, Congressman William Kent and other progressives. Fickert said that the recall movement was the work of anarchists and reds and was endorsed by the chamber of commerce and the Downtown Association. And in a surprise move, the *Chronicle* printed a telegram to Fickert from Theodore Roosevelt:

> *I am informed that an effort is being made to recall you because you successfully prosecuted the anarchists who during the Preparedness Day parade killed ten persons and wounded sixty others. If such be the fact, I not only feel that the issue between you and your opponents is that between patriotism and anarchy, but I also feel that all who directly or indirectly assail you for any such reason should be promptly deprived of citizenship.*
>
> *Anarchist bomb throwers are murderers worse than ordinary murderers, and all men who sympathize with them or give them aid and support are enemies of the country and should at least be disenfranchised, and furthermore, punished to any extent that is necessary.*

Roosevelt's telegram shocked and dismayed Older and his allies. At first, they thought it was fake, and then Older learned that Charles Hanlon, a sponsor of the Preparedness Day parade and Fickert supporter, had asked Roosevelt's old friend Alexander Moore, who knew nothing about the Billings-Mooney cases, to intercede with Roosevelt on Fickert's behalf. Older, Spreckels, Congressman William Kent and other Progressives wired Roosevelt that he had been deceived. But Roosevelt had turned away from his old Progressive allies; in a letter to journalist Chester Rowell, he associated them with violence and even advocated lynching:

> *It is quite impossible that any substantial injustice was done Mooney and Billings…As for Fremont Older, Rudolph Spreckels and Willie Kent, not only do I regard their judgment as hopelessly unsound but I feel they have gradually grown to be downright sympathizers with anarchy and murder, and this to the extent in the case of Older at least of becoming an accessory to the gravest wrongdoing…I feel that it is perfectly clear that Billings and Mooney were among those responsible for the bomb outrages. I am inclined to think that the verdicts are absolutely just, and I am certain that the evidence is such that would warrant and require the execution of both men under the procedure of martial law; and martial law is the proper way for dealing with outrages of this character when it proves impossible to get at the criminals under the ordinary process of civil law.*

The recall campaign got nastier as election day neared. Fickert attacked Older as much as Sweigert, and at one meeting, the candidates almost got into a fistfight. On December 8, the *Bulletin*, under the headline, "Fake Explosion Conspiracy to Save Fickert," repeated an earlier story that someone on Fickert's side was going to set off a dynamite explosion, like the one on Preparedness Day, to divert attention from the issues and create sympathy for Fickert. The *Bulletin* had gotten an anonymous letter, something it did not usually print, but it made an exception as this was "possibly an honest warning which should be made public":

> *I have knowledge that there is to be done some such act as took place at Steuart and Market streets by the present District Attorney's followers and supporters, to retain him in office. A fake dynamiting and an assault upon one of our public officials, that suspicion will immediately fall upon those interested in the bomb-trial cases, is planned…*

You will not make any mistake by giving these matters further publication, and you may be rendering a great service to those whom you are fighting for, that they might at least be given a fair trial in our courts of law and justice.

Late in the evening of the Monday before the election, there was a tremendous explosion outside the east wing of the governor's mansion in Sacramento. Windows were shattered all throughout the building and for blocks around. A hole three feet square was blown in the brick foundation, and all Sacramento was awakened. Governor Stephens and his wife, asleep on the second floor, were unharmed. The person or persons responsible were never found. Fifty-three IWW members were arrested, but no evidence was produced against them and there were no convictions. The only lead was turned up by a former federal detective, who found that a former operative of Martin Swanson's, a man named Clawson, had been a watchman at the Capitol building, had lied about his whereabouts on the night of the explosion, had quit his job shortly afterward and had been seen with Swanson on the day of the explosion.

Turnout for off-year elections is usually light, and San Francisco registrar of voters Harry Zemansky had predicted that 60,000 voters would go to the polls. On election morning, however, it was obvious that even more were going, which Zemansky attributed to the Sacramento bomb. Fickert won easily, 46,460 to Sweigert's 26,983, and sent a telegram to Roosevelt: "Patriotism has triumphed over anarchy." He would run for governor in 1918.

Late in 1917, American labor troubles were threatening the war effort and America's reputation with its allies. The Wilson administration organized a special labor commission to visit troubled areas, meet with labor and management and make recommendations. The Federal Mediation Commission, as it was called, consisted of Secretary of Labor William Wilson, two union labor men, two employers and a counsel, Harvard Law professor Felix Frankfurter. Before leaving Washington, the commission met with President Wilson at the White House. President Wilson had heard that German propagandists were using the Billings-Mooney case to discredit the United States, and he said, "There's one more matter I want this commission to look into and, as the lawyer of the commission, Mr. Frankfurter, this will be particularly your concern. That is the Mooney case which is greatly disturbing to our allies, Russia and Italy. When you get to California, I hope you will look into the matter and report to me about it."

It was the first Frankfurter had heard of Mooney; he thought Mooney was Russian or Italian. After learning that he was from San Francisco, Frankfurter asked some colleagues for information and found that they considered the case too hot to handle. By the time the commission arrived in San Francisco, Frankfurter had learned details from G.S. Arnold, a son-in-law of Congressman Kent. In San Francisco, Supreme Court justice Henshaw and other justices explained the dilemma as they saw it: they couldn't do anything, such as granting Attorney General Webb's request, because they could only go on the record before trial judge Griffin; Griffin couldn't do anything because the case had left his jurisdiction ten days after he imposed sentence; and the Supreme Court had no authority to deal with disclosures—such as the Oxman letters—that would undermine the verdict. Hence, only the governor could grant relief, but so far he hadn't been asked to. Frankfurter read briefs by McNutt and Cockran and met with Arnold, Fickert and Ferrari. He also went to the home of Archbishop Joseph Hannah for a dinner at which many influential churchmen were present. After dinner, the other guests discreetly left Frankfurter alone with the archbishop. They discussed bad labor—management relations in California—and then Archbishop Hannah told Frankfurter, "I know Tom Mooney very well. He and his family were parishioners of mine. Tom is a bad man, but he didn't do this." Frankfurter also met Mooney, who kept Frankfurter waiting while he shaved.

The commission discovered how bitter the Billings-Mooney case was. Some prosecution supporters even conceded that prosecution testimony was perjured but that it didn't matter. As Cunha had said, Billings, Mooney and the others should be in jail because of who they were, guilty or not. Back in Washington, Frankfurter prepared a report. It did not speculate whether Billings and Mooney were guilty or innocent, but it did note that Martin Swanson and the utility companies were behind the prosecution. The acquittals of Rena Mooney and Israel Weinberg cast doubt on the convictions of Billings and Mooney. Oxman's acquittal was irrelevant. The letters discredited his testimony, and "when Oxman was discredited the verdict against Mooney was discredited."

The case had ominous implications for foreign relations:

> *However strange or however unexpected it may be, the just disposition of the Mooney case thus affects influences far beyond…California…the feeling of disquietude aroused by the case must be heeded, for…it impairs the faith that our democracy protects the lowliest and even the unworthy*

> *against false accusations. War is fought with moral as well as material resources. We are in this war to vindicate the moral claims of unstained processes of law…These claims must be tempered by the fire of our own devotion to them at home.*
>
> *Your commission therefore respectfully recommends in case the Supreme Court of California should find it necessary to sustain the conviction of Mooney on the record of the trial, that the President use his good offices to invoke action by the governor of California…to the end that a new trial may be had for Mooney…This result can easily be accomplished by postponing the execution of the sentence of Mooney to await the outcome of a new trial, based upon prosecution under one of the untried indictments against him.*

All the members signed the report, and on January 22, 1918, it was given to President Wilson. On January 26, Wilson wrote to Governor Stephens:

> *Will you permit a suggestion from me in these troubled times…Would it not be possible to postpone the execution of…Mooney until he can be tried upon one of the other indictments against him, in order to give full… consideration to the important changes which I understand to have taken place in the evidence against him?*
>
> *I urge this very respectfully indeed…because the case has assumed international importance and I feel free to make the suggestion because I am sure that you are as anxious as anyone…to have no doubt or…criticism… attach itself to the case.*

The *Bulletin* printed the report the same day. Mooney's defense was jubilant. "The commission's report," said McNutt, "will cause even the most prejudiced to halt and raise in his own mind an honest doubt about the issue." O'Connor said, "We knew there could be but one result…No unbiased man…could possibly have studied the evidence in these cases without being convinced that a terrible miscarriage of justice had taken place." Mooney was awakened in his cell by a jailer and told the news. Prisoners in the cellblock with Weinberg cheered, and the jailers didn't stop them.

Fickert had told the commission that he wanted to file a response to briefs by McNutt and Cockran, but two months passed without one. On January 27, Fickert claimed that the commission had never met with any of the prosecution, only the defense, and said, "I do not mean to become a party to turning loose upon the community…a band of guilty murderers, anarchists and traitors on the recommendation of any commission that has made absolutely no investigation." Dunne said that the report was what he would have expected from "Bolsheviki Frankfurter." In March, Fickert would claim again that Fremont Older bore some kind of responsibility for the bombing, and in July, he would say that Frankfurter had told him that he was satisfied that Mooney had had a fair trial and was guilty, and that he, Frankfurter, was requesting a new trial for Mooney just to placate radicals. That was too much for Frankfurter. After getting confirmation from three Supreme Court justices that he had said no such thing, he telegrammed Governor Stephens:

> *I cannot believe that a district attorney…should willingly or recklessly charge others with facts which he must know to be untrue…I burden you with this telegram of denial in order to avoid even the most remote possibility of misunderstanding.*

Demonstrations on behalf of Mooney, and sometimes Billings, spread in the United States and the world. Labor now considered Mooney a martyr, and July 28, 1918, would be observed as "Mooney Day" in twenty-five American cities. In Derby, England, the September 1918 meeting of the Trades Union Congress resolved to send a telegram to President Wilson to "avoid a grave miscarriage of justice." In Scotland, the Ironmoulders Union asked the British cabinet to demand a new trial for Mooney. A Glasgow branch of the Independent Labour Party said that Mooney's execution would "be a crime equal to any of the atrocities committed during the war." Labor organizations protested in Ireland, Australia and Italy. In Holland, guards were placed around American Legation buildings at The Hague after threats from revolutionary socialists.

In Russia, the Bolsheviks had ousted Kerensky's provisional government, and Lenin had taken power. Anarchists, however, were still a force, and in January 1918, a Petrograd anarchist newspaper told American ambassador Charles Francis that

> [t]*he leading fighter in the cause of liberating mankind, our comrade Thomas Mooney, has been sentenced to death by your government… Russian workmen, peasants, soldiers and sailors have expressed their energetic protest regarding atrocities perpetuated by your government towards honest revolutionists and demanded their immediate liberation. In numerous resolutions regarding this the Russians soldiers, workmen and sailors pointed out that to violence they will reply by violence, to death*

> *by death…we are authorized to officially announce to you that if in the shortest time possible our comrades…will not be liberated then we shall consider you personally responsible for their lives and liberty.*

That was a direct threat to Francis's life, and he took it seriously and went into hiding. If Mooney were to hang and Francis dragged from the American embassy and executed in revenge, the repercussions could have been catastrophic: conservatives in America were agitating for war against the new Soviet Union, and the execution of an ambassador would be an excuse to go to one. It would be the worst consequence of the Billings-Mooney case yet, involving the United States and Europe in another war.

After Mooney's conviction, Fickert had claimed that he would try more than seventy defendants for the Preparedness Day bombing, but by the end of 1917, he had tried only Billings, Tom and Rena Mooney and Israel Weinberg. Superior Court judge George Cabaniss ordered Assistant District Attorney Ferrari to begin Weinberg's next trial on February 13, 1918, and after another delay, Ferrari moved to dismiss two indictments. Cunha was responsible for five more and moved to dismiss those also. In March 1918, the California Supreme Court admitted Weinberg to bail after twenty months in jail. He took his family to Cleveland, Ohio—where he had met his wife after emigrating from Russia—worked as a carpenter and prospered as a contractor. He was never tried in San Francisco again. After Weinberg was released, McNutt filed habeas corpus for Rena Mooney's release. Judge Dunne, although he still believed that all the defendants belonged in jail, agreed to Rena's bail. She was never tried again either.

The same March, the California Supreme Court reaffirmed Mooney's conviction, as it found no error in the trial. Years later, Justice Victor Shaw said that had he been a juror, he would not have voted to convict. The prosecution witnesses were questionable, and the photograph of the Mooneys on the Eilers Building was an alibi. Shaw felt that Mooney was convicted because of his reputation and because of the emotions aroused by the bombing, but under California law, the court had no choice but to reaffirm. The court's decision, like so many others in Billings-Mooney, has since been roundly criticized. In 1965, California Supreme Court justice Raymond Peters said that the decision was absurd: if no precedent existed, the court was justified in created a precedent to set the conviction aside.

McNutt next petitioned trial judge Griffin for *Coram nobis*, an obscure English common law writ used to correct errors of justice when there is no other remedy. Griffin reluctantly ruled that the writ did not apply, and two months later, the Supreme Court upheld him. Griffin said, "I am loath to sentence this man to death," but early in June 1918, he signed the warrant setting Mooney's execution for Friday, August 23. That evening, a court officer entered Griffin's chambers and found him hunched over his desk, his head on his arms, crying.

On June 13, Fickert announced his candidacy for governor. His slogan was "Patriotism or Anarchy," and he would campaign on a platform of having prosecuted the Preparedness Day defendants and of suppressing sedition. Incumbent governor Stephens was colorless, but he had the advantage of being able to deal with the Mooney case. The problem was that he would offend conservatives if he pardoned Mooney, and he would alienate labor and the left if he let him hang. On July 27, one day before Mooney Day, Stephens said that he was commuting Mooney's execution until Friday, December 13, 1918. Stephens said that commutation was not a political move and that he had done it because he needed to study the case, but by delaying the execution until after election day, he took the Billings-Mooney issue out of the campaign.

The Densmore Report

By mid-1918, Fremont Older's situation at the *Bulletin* had gone from bad to worse. Older had rescued it from ruin in 1895 and made his publisher, Crothers, wealthy. But Crothers's nephew, Loring Pickering Jr., now in his majority, sought social recognition, according to Older, and with a substantial fortune, he was an eligible male among the fashionable set. The questionable glory of a crusade to release two innocent labor men from prison because they were convicted by perjury was an interference.

The *Bulletin* was also facing serious competition for the first time since Older had become managing editor. The *Morning Call*, named after a popular stage play, was one of San Francisco's oldest newspapers in continual production, having begun in 1856, a year after the evening *Bulletin*. Mark Twain was briefly a reporter until he was fired, and Older had been the *Call*'s city editor until Crothers offered

Bulletin publisher Robert ("R.A.") Crothers, circa 1900. *Author's collection.*

him the managing editor position of the *Bulletin*. Facing strong competition from the morning *Examiner*, owned by William Randolph Hearst, and the *Chronicle*, owned by the de Young family, the *Call*'s circulation had dropped in the early twentieth century. In 1913, the *Call*'s owner, John D. Spreckels—the grand jury foreman at the time of the Mooney case—had sold the *Call*, and it had become an afternoon paper. The nominal buyer was one F.W. Kellogg, but the real owner was William Randolph Hearst. Under Kellogg's management, the *Call* had merged with the afternoon *Post* in 1913, boosting circulation. Hearst, as was his practice, threw his considerable financial resources into the afternoon *Call and Post* and was muscling in on *Bulletin* territory in more ways than one: there were street fights between *Bulletin* and *Call* vendors.

Publication of the Oxman letters brought matters to a head at the *Bulletin*. Either Crothers or Pickering, probably the former but certainly with the latter's backing, ordered Older to stop fighting on Mooney's and Billings's behalf. "But such an order is often more easily given than carried out," Older wrote later. "The enormity of the injustice that had been committed was so great that every member of the staff of the *Bulletin* was indignant that such a just fight should be suddenly abandoned. Encouraged by the men and women employed on the paper, I continued to publish the results of further investigations into the corrupt practices of those in charge of the prosecution."

"The situation became exceedingly tense." Crothers and Pickering were ordered to appear before the Law and Order Committee. Older asked to accompany them, but they refused, as it was their property in jeopardy, not his. From what they told Older afterward, it was a sorry spectacle. They made no attempt to defend the paper but instead pleaded for mercy and forgiveness, promised not to offend further and, incidentally, absolved themselves by blaming Older—he was very impetuous and easily misled into advocating dangerous causes. In early summer, they gave Older an ultimatum: drop the Mooney (and Billings) case or be fired. It was the darkest moment of Older's life. He was sixty-two, and he and Cora had a mortgage. If he dropped the case, Mooney would probably hang, and Billings would die in prison. If he didn't drop the case and was fired, Mooney and Billings would suffer the same fates anyway.

Then, out of a clear sky came a telegram from William Randolph Hearst:

> *Come to the Call. Bring the Mooney Case with You.*

It seemed surreal. Older speculated later whether thoughts travel—had Hearst received a message? In fact, he may have, though not telepathically. Newspaper people are notorious gossips, so Hearst may have heard of Older's predicament at the *Bulletin*. In fact, Hearst had been trying to hire Older away from Crothers for years, which Older resisted as he valued his independence, but he used Hearst's interest in him as leverage to induce Crothers to raise his salary. The Billings-Mooney case gave Hearst the leverage *he* needed.

Older did not accept Hearst's offer immediately. In July, he asked Pickering for a contract, but Pickering wrote to him that it was impossible. Older then penned a letter to Crothers, but equally intended for Pickering:

> *San Francisco, California*
> *July 16th, 1918*
>
> *Dear Mr. Crothers:*
>
> *I wish to resign my position as Managing Editor of The Bulletin, and I should like the resignation to take effect immediately, as my temporary continuance, as representative of policies with which you are less and less in sympathy, would be of no real value to the paper.*
>
> *More than two years ago you began to show hostility to nearly all of my activities as Managing Editor, and the feeling grew upon me, from day to day and week to week, that there was very little left that I could do to hold the paper to the course it had pursued for many years. In arbitrarily altering the policies that I believe have been the heart and soul of The Bulletin since the graft prosecutions, you have, in my judgment, made it impossible for a big newspaper to hold the confidence of the people. Thought throughout the world is rapidly changing. Democracy may soon cease to be the comfortable, meaningless, and empty phrase it has been in the past. It may come to have a real meaning; it may gather force and power, and rather quickly bring about a readjustment of the economic inequalities which now exist all over the world. In that event, even the advanced policies of The Bulletin of a few years ago, which are now forbidden by you, would be regarded as mere commonplaces by a world awakened to the realities and to the injustices that all through the centuries have been the lot of the common man.*
>
> *Intellectually and emotionally, I have been deeply interested in the old policies of The Bulletin. While they may have been crude and faltering, and still clouded by misunderstanding—the parent of hate and intolerance—I believe they contain something of the message that should go out to all mankind. But, even thou I had chosen them as a matter of economic*

expediency, and had held the same views on labor and capital that you do, my newspaper judgment would still have compelled me to hold the paper firmly in the path it had been traveling for so many years. But you willed that there should be no further advocacy of, or sympathy with, the causes that had grown so dear to me. You had a legal property right to make this decision. I have at all times recognized that right; but, while recognizing, I continued for a long time to hope that I might be able to persuade you at least to let a dim light burn in The Bulletin window—not to snuff it out as you have done, and leave us in utter darkness. Even though I have thus far failed to convince you that should be more in accord with my views, I feel that our close personal relations, extending through so many years, might have inclined you, though unconvinced, to yield somewhat to my views, and I might go on with the struggle, if I had you alone to deal with. But the influence of your nephew is growing upon the conduct of The Bulletin. He now owns a one-quarter interest, and will ultimately own it all. As you well know, he is hostile to me and to everything that I represent. If you were in full agreement with me as to policies, I doubt if you would have the strength to control him, much less when your views are so nearly in accord with his. Thus my usefulness to you is at an end.

I do not blame you for your attitude of mind. No doubt you are honestly convinced that you are right, and you are by no means alone in your belief. Most of those who are comfortably placed in life agree with you. I cannot. It may be that the old policies of the paper, which are so dear to me, were only dreams, but they have taken such a firm hold upon my imagination that I must cling to them to the end. I have gone too far now to turn back. I should get lost on the way.

Parting from you and The Bulletin after twenty-four years of intimate association is a tragedy, but I see no other course.

Sincerely yours,
Fremont Older.

Crothers was dismayed but consoled himself with the thought that he would save $10,000 per year on Older's salary. Fremont and Cora Older took a train to New York to confer with Hearst, who asked Older if he would consider being editor of his *New York Journal*. Settled in California, Older preferred the *Call*. The Olders returned to San Francisco, where Fremont took up his duties at the *Call* on August 19, 1918. His new office was at 74 New Montgomery Street, just across narrow Jessie Street south of the Palace Hotel. *Bulletin* editorial writer Robert Duffus gave his resignation to Crothers, who asked sullenly if he was going with Older. Duffus answered evasively, but in fact that's just what he did. Other *Bulletin* staffers did likewise or went elsewhere.

Congratulations on Older's taking up the *Call* editorship poured into the paper. Publisher F.W. Kellogg wrote a lengthy editorial reviewing the paper's history, including an earlier attempt to hire Older and the reasons why:

> *As editor of the San Francisco Bulletin he had by more than twenty-five* [sic] *years of continuous, constant, and consistent newspaper work secured for the Bulletin a very large following…*
>
> *Fremont Older was the best loved and most bitterly denounced of any citizen of San Francisco, but friend or foe alike always stated or admitted that Fremont Older was honest in his beliefs, courageous in advocating them…His following, or rather the people who believed in him, were so numerous that he has for years been denounced by all profiteers from special privilege, and their unthinking associates and beneficiaries, and by many superficially informed citizens, as the most dangerous man in San Francisco.*
>
> *"Dangerous," and why? Because thousands of people believed in him, had learned to trust his vision and guidance, rely upon his courage and defense, and love him for the human understanding that has not permitted him to forget the many meek and lowly of this world. And public and private profiteers from special privileges are prone to fear any honest journalist with a real following of thousands of believing subscribers.*

An explanation by Older of his reasons for leaving the *Bulletin* and coming to the *Call* followed. In a paragraph on the *Bulletin*'s dynamics, he referred to Loring Pickering, though not by name, just as "the young man heir." Everyone in San Francisco, of course, knew whom he meant. He included a paragraph on Billings-Mooney:

> *I took up the Mooney case, not because Mooney was a good man or a bad one, but because he had not had an honest trial. I believed, as I still believe, that if all that has been said against Mooney were true, it is still just as important that he should have a fair trial as that the richest or most prominent man should have one. It is even more important, for millions of men here and in other countries need to be convinced that the courts of a political democracy will give the poor as fair a chance as they give the rich. With President Wilson's help, in the middle of a great war, the profound significance of this case has been made manifest, but it would have been profoundly significant under any circumstances.*

Fremont Older, circa 1919, about a year after he became *Call* editor. *Donna and Earl Harris.*

The relationship between Hearst and Older has been much discussed. Many of Older's subscribers were dismayed that he went to work for Hearst after so many years opposing him. Older, on the other hand, would say that the years of working for Hearst were the happiest of his life. Cora would write flattering biographies of both William Randolph and his father, Senator George Hearst. Correspondence between Hearst and Older suggests that they had a respectful relationship, though not a close friendship. They addressed each other formally—"Mr. Hearst" and "Mr. Older"—rather than by first names. In any case, Hearst promised Older that he could have an independent editorial policy at the *Call*, which Older had.

The California gubernatorial primary election was on Tuesday, August 27. Incumbent governor Stephens had cross-filed on the Republican, Progressive and Prohibition ballots. His main opponent was San Francisco mayor Rolph, who cross-filed on the Democratic and Republican ballots. Rolph ran first with 221,945 total votes, but because Stephens had more Republican votes—168,942 to Rolph's 146,990—he won the Republican nomination. As Rolph was a Republican, he could not qualify for the Democratic nomination without also winning the Republican one, so Stephens would win in November by default. To the relief of the Mooney defense, Fickert ran eighth out of nine Republican candidates, with just over 13,000 votes.

About the time of the November election, Older had a visit from Lieutenant Charles Goff of the police department and one George Parson, a federal investigator whom Older had never met. Parson told Older that when the Federal Mediation Committee was in San Francisco, Secretary of Labor Wilson had requested John B. Densmore, Department of Labor solicitor, to investigate the Billings-Mooney case. Densmore had Fickert shadowed and had two operatives posing as telephone technicians get into Fickert's office in the Hall of Justice and install secret microphones on the telephone lines, recording all incoming and outgoing calls. The calls, from two periods—June and September to late October—were transcribed and included in a bulky report, with Densmore's comments. *Call* reporter Edgar ("Scoop") Gleeson had also been shadowing Fickert and knew about the other shadow, but Older and Gleeson thought that it was someone working for Fickert's wife. Fickert patronized prostitutes, sometimes two or three per day, and his wife was considering divorce. Parson had come to ask Older not to print anything about the investigation before it was complete, to which Older agreed. When the investigation was finished late in November, Parson delivered a voluminous report to Older.

The Densmore Report, as it would be known, appeared Friday, November 22, 1918. World War I had ended less than two weeks earlier, and international

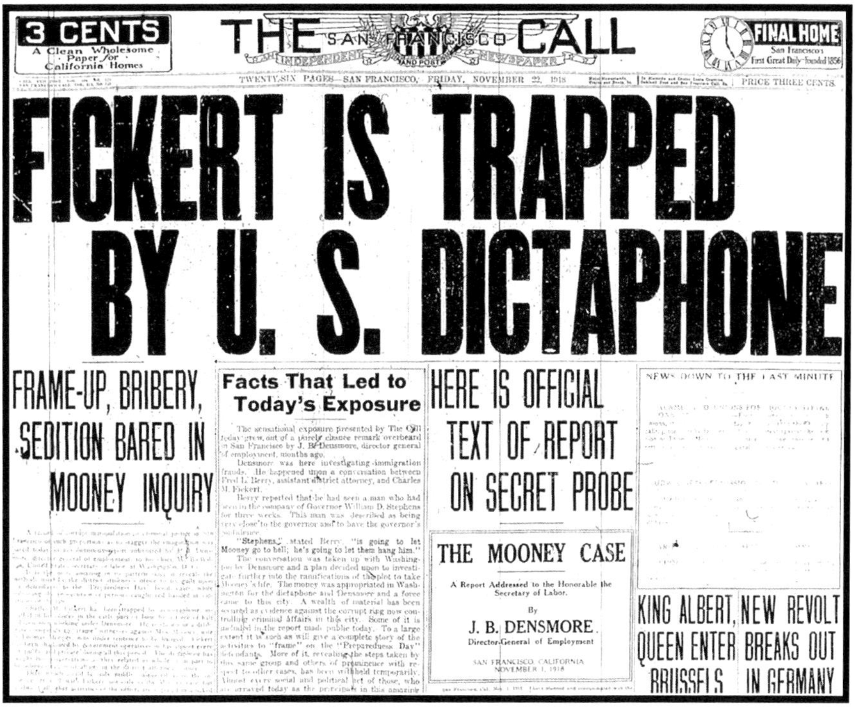

3 CENTS
A Clean Wholesome Paper for California Homes

THE SAN FRANCISCO CALL
INDEPENDENT AND POST NEWSPAPER

FINAL HOME
San Francisco's First Great Daily—Founded 1856

TWENTY-SIX PAGES—SAN FRANCISCO, FRIDAY, NOVEMBER 22, 1918 | PRICE THREE CENTS

FICKERT IS TRAPPED BY U. S. DICTAPHONE

FRAME-UP, BRIBERY, SEDITION BARED IN MOONEY INQUIRY

Facts That Led to Today's Exposure

The sensational exposure presented by The Call today grew out of a purely chance remark overheard in San Francisco by J. B. Densmore, director general of employment, months ago.

Densmore was here investigating immigration frauds. He happened upon a conversation between Fred L. Berry, assistant district attorney, and Charles M. Fickert.

Berry reported that he had seen a man who had been in the company of Governor William D. Stephens for three weeks. This man was described as being very close to the governor and to have the governor's confidence.

"Stephens," stated Berry, "is going to let Mooney go to hell; he's going to let them hang him."

The conversation was taken up with Washington by Densmore and a plan decided upon to investigate further into the ramifications of the plot to take Mooney's life. The money was appropriated in Washington for the dictaphone and Densmore and a force came to this city. A wealth of material has been secured as evidence against the corrupt ring now controlling criminal affairs in this city. Some of it is included in the report made public today. To a large extent it is such as will give a complete story of the activities to "frame" on the "Preparedness Day" defendants. More of it, revealing the steps taken by this same group and others of prominence with respect to other cases, has been withheld temporarily. Almost every social and political act of those, who are arrayed today as the principals in this amazing

HERE IS OFFICIAL TEXT OF REPORT ON SECRET PROBE

THE MOONEY CASE
A Report Addressed to the Honorable the Secretary of Labor.
By
J. B. DENSMORE
Director-General of Employment
SAN FRANCISCO, CALIFORNIA
NOVEMBER 1, 1918

NEWS DOWN TO THE LAST MINUTE

KING ALBERT, QUEEN ENTER BRUSSELS

NEW REVOLT BREAKS OUT IN GERMANY

The *Call* announces the Densmore Report, November 22, 1918.

news dominated headlines, but the first eight pages of the *Call* were almost entirely about the report. Fickert's malfeasance in office was laid bare: he had been recorded arranging with a bail bondsman to fix cases and release arrested persons, for a price. It was revealed that Mooney's prosecution was dictated by Frank Drew, attorney for the chamber of commerce, and by Frederick C. Henshaw, a former justice of the California Supreme Court.

The Densmore Report did not, as Billings and Mooney's adherents would claim, prove that the prosecution had knowingly used perjured testimony, but it did show conclusively, among other things, that Fickert and Cunha were planning to. The *Call* for Saturday, November 23, had an account by reporter Elenore Meherin of how the district attorney was going to entrap one Mrs. Virginia Judd, whose husband, Norris, owned a printing and binding firm. The Judds lived at 49 Park Hill Avenue, a nice address just southeast of Buena Vista Park. Mrs. Judd had no involvement with Billings-Mooney, but her sister Mrs. Lillian Barlow was in contact with a detective named Otts who had promised Fickert to get witnesses. Virginia Judd had seen Otts's picture and disliked his looks, but around October 1, 1918, she had a telephone call from him. Otts said that he was making a movie and that Mrs. Judd, a prominent woman, would be a nice addition to it. Mrs. Judd thought his proposal ridiculous. Her husband said to hang up on Otts if he called again, which he did. Then Otts called at the Judds' house. The plot, as recorded conversations in the Densmore Report revealed, was to get Mrs. Judd to Buena Vista Park, where a man was waiting in the shrubbery. The man would grab Mrs. Judd in a compromising position as a photograph was taken. The photograph would be used to blackmail her into testifying that she had seen Rena Mooney at Market and Steuart Streets. The dictaphone recorded Cunha's and Fickert's plans:

> *Cunha: "Chief, if you can get a witness who will put Mrs. Mooney at Steuart and Market, I don't give a damn if you put her there in a balloon."*
> *Fickert: "I think we can put her there in a taxicab. It looks as though we have the witness."*
> *Cunha: "If you have, Chief, I will put that son-of-a-bitch* [sic] *Mrs. Mooney on trial again and I will convict her by every rule of the game."*

Revelations in the Densmore Report were particularly damning to former California Supreme Court justice Frederick Henshaw. In 1894, James G. Fair, one of the Nevada silver king millionaires, died, leaving an estate of about $45 million. Fair was divorced but had one living son, Charles, and two daughters, Theresa and Virginia (Theresa married Herman Oelrichs of New York and built the Fairmont Hotel, named after her father). In a classic case of hardworking, wealthy father and dissipate children (in fact, Charles Fair had married a prominent local madam), Fair's will provided for a trust to pay his offspring only interest from his fortune. Charles Fair and his wife were killed racing a Mercedes automobile in France shortly after the elder Fair's death. The daughters sued to have the trust set aside, which would give them access to the entire fortune. The suit went to the California State Supreme Court, which ruled four to three against the heirs.

In 1901, the court granted the heirs a petition for rehearing. The swing vote was Henshaw, who also changed his vote in the final decision in favor of the heirs. In 1917, a man named William Dingee came to Older with a story that he had been intermediary between Henshaw and the Fair heirs. The heirs paid installments totaling $400,000 into an account at the First National Bank of San Francisco. Dingee entered them under the name J. Brown into a ledger, which showed Henshaw withdrawing the money. He executed a document detailing the transactions and gave it to Older to publish.

Older did not publish immediately, as Crothers, who had an old-fashioned courtesy concerning fellow members of the legal profession, did not want to expose Henshaw. Henshaw heard somehow about the documents and said that he would kill Older if he published, and then he asked Older to come to his chambers. Older said instead that he would meet him at Henshaw's apartment at the Fairmont. Henshaw at first claimed that someone had learned in advance of his intention to change his vote and had just sold the information to the Fair heirs.

Supreme Court justice Frederick Henshaw, who took a $400,000 bribe from the heirs of James Fair to break his will. *Author's collection.*

"That isn't true," replied Older. "I happen to know from Dingee's ledger that you received the money for your decision." It was a shock to Henshaw, as he thought the ledger had been destroyed along with so many other records in the earthquake and fire of April 1906, but in fact, they were taken to Mill Valley, California, just prior. The next morning, Henshaw had a proposition. If Older would promise not to publish, Henshaw would resign from the Supreme Court, saying that he wanted to do war work; would try to get the governor to grant Mooney a new trial; and would sever connections with Fickert and Mooney's prosecution.

Henshaw resigned, but the Densmore Report showed him reneging on his promise to sever ties with Fickert, with whom he stayed in regular contact about prosecuting Mooney. On Saturday, November 23, the *Call* printed the story of Henshaw's being bribed $400,000, with images of the journal entries. On the twenty-fifth, lawyer F.H. Dam wrote to Older:

> *Henshaw may deny until he is black in the face; no one will believe him. Your narration of the facts is convincing. "Henshaw's flop" has been a frequent topic of discussion ever since it occurred on April 30, 1901. I have heard lawyers by the dozens say they believe Henshaw was influenced by some consideration other than the "more detailed and exhaustive consideration of the authorities," as he put it in his concurring opinion in 132 Cal. 550. Referring to the "error" of his position on the first hearing...he says that it "came from a failure to give due recognition to the fact emphasized and demonstrated upon the last argument," etc. We are no longer left in doubt as to precisely what the "fact" was...Four hundred thousand dollars is some "fact"...*
>
> *Allow me to thank you for showing up one of the most disgraceful cases of corruption in juridical history. The taint of this makes valueless every decision which Henshaw wrote.*

The Densmore Report was a sensation. It was read into the Congressional Record and reported worldwide. Gratitude such as Dam's, however, was not universal. San Francisco's grand jury demanded some sort of investigation of Densmore, and the Downtown Association threatened to file suit against him. No other newspaper printed the report in its entirety, although Older gave them permission to. On the evening of Sunday, November 24, Older returned to San Francisco and entered the Palace Hotel. On his way through the lobby to the desk to register, he saw Fickert coming toward him, along with Fickert's assistant, Fred Berry, and a third man he did not recognize. As they passed, Fickert swung at Older with both fists. Fickert was a big man, sixteen years younger than Older, and Older was knocked to the floor. Conscious but dazed, he heard Fickert screaming an "unprintable" as he kicked him. Berry pulled Fickert away. Older rose and was helped to a room. Across Jessie Street, *Call* staffers heard that Older had been killed. Grabbing whatever weapons were handy, they charged into Palace after Fickert, but Older intercepted them and sent them back to work. Fickert said afterward that Older had reached in his pocket for a gun.

By tradition, executions at San Quentin took place on Fridays. Mooney's was set, ironically, for Friday the thirteenth in December. On November 28, Thanksgiving Day, Governor Stephens delivered a lengthy statement that included some, but not all, of the correspondence from President Wilson, which was previously secret. In June, Wilson had telegrammed Stephens:

> *I beg that you will believe that I am moved only by a sense of public duty and of consciousness of the many and complicated interests involved when I again must respectfully suggest a commutation of the death sentence imposed upon Mooney. I would not venture again to call your attention to this case did I not know the international significance which attaches to it.*

Stephens made it plain that he had no sympathy for Mooney and considered him a dangerous anarchist, not a labor figure. However, as there seemed to be some doubt in the minds of a few citizens about Mooney's guilt, he was agreeing to Wilson's request and commuted Mooney's sentence to life imprisonment. He did not mention that Wilson had earlier requested a pardon for Mooney, and he said nothing about a new trial. That he commuted Mooney's sentence at all was certainly due at least in part to the Densmore Report.

Stephens's action was denounced most vociferously by Mooney himself in a letter from San Quentin:

> *Governor Stephens: It is my life you are dealing with. I demand that you revoke your commutation of my death sentence to a living death. I prefer a glorious death at the hands of my traducers, you included, to a living grave. I am innocent.*
>
> *I demand a new and fair trial or my unconditional liberty through a pardon. If I were guilty of the crime for which I have been unjustly convicted, hanging would be too good for me. Then why commute my sentence to life.*

Defense attorney Cockran called Stephens's action "stupidity." "How any man who believed Mooney guilty could have commuted his sentence is inconceivable." Felix Frankfurter said that the commutation made no sense: if Mooney was guilty, he should be executed; if innocent, he should be freed; if there was doubt, there should be a new trial.

The first of Frankfurter's three possibilities having been removed, there followed a long, frustrating campaign to bring about one or the other of the next two: pardon or a new trial. Fickert, discredited by the Oxman letters and the Densmore Report, lost the 1919 election for district attorney to Judge Matthew Brady and never held elective office again. Before leaving, he tried to have all remaining indictments against Mooney dismissed. The defense was in the peculiar position of arguing for keeping the indictments open, as a new trial, and acquittal, would free Mooney. Judge Griffin agreed to retain one indictment each against Billings and Mooney.

Pardon was out of the question for the foreseeable future. Stephens was governor until 1922, and he would do nothing more. The best the defense could do was to keep the case in the public eye and try legal moves until a new governor was elected. At the end of 1918, Mooney was at least no longer under sentence of death, but he and Billings had been in prison for two and a half years.

The Cases Drag On and On and On

On the pages of the *Call*, Older relentlessly continued campaigning for Billings and Mooney. On Friday, November 12, 1920, he held an unusual meeting in his office with police officer Draper Hand, Mayor Rolph and a stenographer. Rolph entered all smiles as usual. Ushering his guests in, Older strategically took a chair between the door and them, trapping Rolph. Hand, who had been involved in the Billings-Mooney case from the start, told a story that "cut the heart out of the prosecution."

When Oregon cattleman Frank Oxman arrived in San Francisco, said Hand, he had never seen Weinberg's jitney—the jitney that Oxman testified Weinberg drove down Market Street during the Preparedness Day parade carrying Billings, Mooney, Rena Mooney and an unidentified fifth person as Mooney held the fatal suitcase on the running board. Prior to the trials, Weinberg's jitney was held at the North End Police Station. Hand was told by Martin Swanson to take Oxman there. "There was no need for explicit orders," noted the *Call*. "I took Oxman to see the car," Hand told Rolph. "It was his first and only sight of the car…Oxman was very much concerned, when he saw the car, to find out if it were possible for a man to sit in it and hold a suitcase as he was going to describe in court. He had me get in the car and let my hand hang down over the side, as if I were holding a suitcase. He wasn't satisfied till I got in and did as he wanted; after that he thought his version was all right—that the defense wouldn't prove it impossible."

The car's license number was another issue, said Hand. Cunha had had the license plate taken off the car. Hand took it from a drawer and copied the number, which was given to Oxman. At trial, Oxman said that when he saw the car at Steuart Street, he wrote down the number, a common practice among ranchers, because he suspected a stolen car.

Rolph was a kindly man, with a constitutional antipathy for nasty messes. Realizing that he was caught in an extremely distasteful situation, his smile froze. Hand continued with an account of John McDonald, who testified seeing Billings and Mooney—but no jitney—at Market and Steuart Streets a few minutes before the bomb exploded. He was given favors, including pocket money, until interest in him began to wane. Finally, he said, "Unless I get a job I'm going to spill everything to Fremont Older." A job was found for him in Tracy, California, about fifty miles east of San Francisco, but he apparently did little or no work.

Estelle Smith had also become a problem for the prosecution, said Hand. Matheson felt that she was given too much attention and that the Edeaus, mother and daughter, would be better witnesses. Hand said that he took the Edeaus to city prison and pointed out Billings, Mooney and Weinberg to them.

When Hand had finished, Older moved from his chair. Rolph bolted from the room and didn't speak to Older for years.

Estelle Smith reappeared in the same edition of the *Call*. She now told District Attorney Brady that she was not sure if Billings was the man she saw in the dentist's office at 721 Market Street. The next day, Saturday, November 13, the *Call* printed another revelation, this one from prosecutor James Brennan. Why Brennan had asked the jury in Billings's trial to impose a life sentence rather than the death penalty had been one of the mysteries of the Billings-Mooney case. Brennan explained why:

> *James F. Brennan, prosecutor of Warren K. Billings, flatly declared today that he would not have voted for conviction had he been sitting as a juror in the case.*
>
> *This sensational statement, following close on Draper Hand's declaration to Mayor Rolph yesterday that the entire Mooney case was a frame-up from start to finish, tore aside the last thin shred to which the prosecution has been desperately clinging to keep Mooney and Billings in prison.*
>
> *Brennan said that the evidence which he himself placed before court and jury was not conclusive...There was and is reasonable doubt as to Billings' connection with the bomb...Brennan did not, and could not, he admitted, actually prove to his own satisfaction that Billings was guilty of the dastardly crime. For that reason he did not ask the death penalty, he said.*

The story continued with Brennan's *mea culpa*:

> *Like all prosecutors, I was blind to all but the pursuit—the case which would end with the conviction of my quarry.*
>
> *I was cursed with the psychology of prosecution. I shall never again be a prosecutor. To my mind, and it is the mind of every district attorney, conviction is the only goal…*
>
> *I would say that, as a general rule, no man wants to put an innocent person in prison. The prosecutor's motives can not in a majority of cases be questioned. But he is biased toward conviction, and this is uppermost in his mind. Every public prosecutor wants to make a record. He sees as his goal political preferment, applause of his constituents, his personal aggrandizement. This can be gained only by conviction of the accused, against whom the public mind in sensational cases has already been poisoned…*
>
> *This case has been a nightmare since the date of the trial…I regard it as an evil day in my life that I was given charge of the prosecution.*

Sensational as Hand's story was, it made no difference legally. As 1920 ended, Billings and Mooney had been in jail for four and a half years.

In January 1921, Captain Duncan Matheson of the police department received a strange letter from Trenton, New Jersey. It was from John McDonald, the itinerant waiter-cum-other-things who had claimed that he had seen two men with a suitcase at Steuart and Market Streets a few minutes before the explosion. At trial, McDonald had identified Billings and Mooney and had previously and unsuccessfully written to Matheson about the reward portion that he was supposed to have gotten but never did. Now, having read in the newspapers about Draper Hand's revelations to Rolph, he wrote to Matheson asking, "What is all the fuss about Mooney again… has Draper Hand gone crazy, I will say on my death bed and the last words from me, would be that he [Mooney] is guilty…and I will swear to what I swore before, the truth."

McDonald was chronically unwell—he may have contracted syphilis—and one month later, he thought he *was* on his deathbed. His tone changed. Appearing in defense attorney Frank Walsh's New York office, he told Walsh that he wanted to make a clean breast of things and would tell the whole truth. A secretary took dictation in affidavit form.

After Preparedness Day, McDonald said, he saw Fickert, who was uninterested in McDonald's description of a man with a dark complexion, thirty to thirty-five years old, five feet, seven or eight inches, about 150 pounds, and another man twenty-five to thirty years old, about five feet, eight inches and 145 pounds, with a medium complexion. "Tom Mooney is the son-of-a-bitch we want," said Fickert, according to McDonald. After Billings and Mooney were arrested, McDonald said that Lieutenant Goff showed him Billings and Mooney in their cells and that Fickert told him he would be paid expenses and would be given the biggest share of the reward.

At Billings's trial, McDonald testified seeing Billings and Mooney at Steuart Street just minutes before 2:00 p.m. Before Mooney's trial, however, he said that Cunha told him to change the time to about 1:30 p.m. The reason, if McDonald's affidavit was truthful, was that the photos of Tom and Rena Mooney on the Eilers Building roof, with a street clock showing one minute past two. Mooney's alleged presence at Steuart Street at 1:30 p.m. would supposedly have left him time—this is questionable—to get back to the Eilers Building. McDonald worried that the defense attorney would spot the contradiction. "Oh, hell," said Cunha, "we will beat him on that. You can say that you were not positive about it at the time of the first trial."

Accompanied by Jack Johnston of the Chicago Federation of Labor, McDonald took the train to Sacramento and drove to San Jose, but a scheduled hearing before San Francisco's grand jury never materialized due to the possibility that McDonald might be indicted for perjury in the Mooney trial. He returned to Baltimore and obscurity.

In about the spring of 1918, another witness came to light. When Oxman said that he took the train to San Francisco from Northern California, it was after he had visited one Earl Hatcher and wife in Woodland, California, about ninety miles north of San Francisco. He said that he had arrived in arrived in San Francisco at about 1:30 p.m., when the parade had just begun. In 1918, Hatcher told a San Francisco attorney named Charles H. Sooy that Oxman was not telling the truth. He looked at Hatcher's livestock on the morning of July 22, had lunch with the Hatchers and took a nap. Hatcher walked Oxman to the Woodland train station, where Oxman boarded some time—the train schedules were later changed—after 2:00 p.m.

Sooy told Fremont Older about Hatcher's admission. Unfortunately, Hatcher had previously testified at Oxman's perjury trial that Oxman had boarded in Woodland just after 9:00 a.m. Possibly he wanted to keep Oxman's friendship and business dealings with him. Later in 1918, however, Hatcher was in dire financial stress. Believing that Oxman owed him a favor, he asked for a loan. Oxman turned him down. Hatcher turned bitter against Oxman and told Oxman's lawyer in Oregon that he had lied earlier and that Oxman could not have reached San Francisco before 5:00 p.m. (Hatcher's bitterness against Oxman would be used to discredit his testimony years later.) In May 1921, Hatcher and his wife testified before San Francisco's grand jury that Oxman had lied, but it preferred to believe his earlier testimony.

Another revelation arrived in July 1922. Mrs. Carrie MacNevin, whose husband, William, was jury foreman in the Mooney trial, sued him for divorce. She also filed an affidavit stating that William MacNevin and Edward Cunha were friendly, so much so that they met secretly in the evenings during the trial. MacNevin suggested to Cunha how to influence certain jurors; Cunha gave MacNevin information on Mooney's background that MacNevin mentioned during deliberations. Nonetheless, by the mid-1920s, all living jurors, MacNevin included, would say that they were convinced that Mooney had not planted the bomb. Oxman's testimony, and only Oxman's testimony, had decided them, and it had been completely discredited. Judge Griffin, for his part, called the Mooney case one of the dirtiest ever put up and resented having had his court used in it.

One of the strangest things about the Billings-Mooney case was the seeming inability of the law—or how it was interpreted—to remedy an obvious injustice. In May 1921, the defense reached all the way back to fourteenth-century English common law, applying to Superior Court judge Harold Louderback for *audita querela* ("the complaint having been heard"), an obscure writ used to quash a judgment when a new defense arose after judgment has been rendered. A hearing, which Mooney attended, was held before Louderback, attorneys Byron Parker and Thomas Wickes appearing for the defense and Milton U'Ren for the district attorney. It was conceded by everyone that injustice had been done, but Louderback denied the application, *audita querela* not being available in California.

In 1922, William Stephens lost the gubernatorial primary election to Friend Richardson, after which Stephens was a lame duck with nothing to lose by pardoning Mooney, but he declined an appeal by Older to do so. Richardson was a conservative with no sympathy for any prisoner, but as all available legal moves had failed, the defense prepared a lengthy pardon application. The application was accompanied by a impressive list of letters from individuals involved in Mooney's conviction: Judge Griffin, District Attorney Brady, nine of the ten surviving jurors (including Cunha's friend, MacNevin), former assistant district attorney Brennan and Officers Matheson and Goff (Matheson, like Older, had concluded that Oxman had deep psychological problems). In November 1926, however, Richardson was defeated for renomination by Clement Calhoun ("C.C." Young); the petition was not submitted until December, and Richardson, saying that he desired to be fair, declined to review the application and left it for his successor. As the year ended, Billings and Mooney had been in jail for ten and a half years.

Young was a glimmer of hope for the defense. He had graduated Phi Beta Kappa from the University of California–Berkeley, had taught English at San Francisco's elite Lowell High School, was a Progressive ally of Older's and was one of Hiram Johnson's first backers in 1910. He had retained links with Progressives, had been speaker of the Assembly and was twice elected lieutenant governor. But he was not Hiram Johnson, and after World War I, California and the United States entered one of those repressive eras that follow progressive ones. In 1919, the legislature passed the Criminal Syndicalism Law, which was used to suppress labor demonstrations (author Upton Sinclair was arrested under the law in 1923 for reading the First Amendment to the Constitution of the United States aloud after police warned him to "cut out that Constitution stuff"). In 1927, Young pardoned Charlotte Anita Whitney, a radical from a prominent family who had been convicted of criminal syndicalism for being a Communist Party member. One such case seemed enough for Young. In August 1927, journalist Chester Rowell wrote to Fremont Older:

> *I will be very glad to seek the opportunity to talk to Governor Young about the Mooney case at whatever psychological moment it would seem to do any good. My own impression is, however, that he would at this time be inclined to stand so straight as to lean backward in order to square himself with those who were horrified at his pardon of Miss Whitney…Logically, the two cases have no relation, but psychologically, they arouse the same emotions. Having made good with the soft hearted, like you and me…I have a notion that the Governor's impulse would be to make good with the "hard boiled" in his next decision…*
>
> *So far as I can find out, the only people who want* [Mooney] *kept in the penitentiary are those who neither know nor care whether he is guilty of the particular crime of which he was convicted, but who think he ought to be locked up on general principles for the other crimes and general undesirable character which they attribute to him…I think there is a very great injustice to the social structure and to the self-respect of democracy when it allows its machinery to be used for that purpose.*

Young suggested to Older and McNutt that Mooney apply for parole, which Mooney had repeatedly said he would never accept, as parole was for the guilty;

Mooney wanted nothing less than for the State of California to acknowledge that he was innocent. Young also told Rowell that the agitation for Mooney was because of his "prominence in former years as a rather militant dissenter from the established order of things, rather than for causes immediately connected with his trial." On September 28, 1927, Older wrote to Young. His tone was respectful, but his impatience and sarcasm showed through:

> *My Dear Governor Young:*
>
> *Chester Rowell let me know your attitude on the Mooney case, as revealed to him in a letter…That you would not pardon Mooney but might permit him to be paroled did not come as a complete surprise to me, as I had heard such a rumor from several reliable sources.*
>
> *I was, however, surprised to learn that you had brought yourself to believe that whatever appeal had been made in Mooney's interests was largely because of his prominence in former years as a rather militant dissenter from the established order of things, rather than for causes immediately connected with his trial.*
>
> *I certainly know of no one who is interested in the injustice being done to Mooney who has been influenced by their admiration for Mooney's activities prior to the bomb explosion. Certainly President Wilson could not have been so influenced when he urged Governor Stephens to commute his sentence from death to life imprisonment…The President sent Mr. Frankfurter to California to find out the facts, and it was upon those facts that President Wilson based his plea for commutation of Mooney's sentence.*
>
> *I am quite sure that Judge Griffin, who tried the Mooney case, was only influenced by his knowledge that Oxman, the pivotal witness in the Mooney trial, had committed perjury, and that Oxman was not in the city when the bomb exploded but was in Woodland waiting for the 2:10 PM train. The bomb exploded at 2:06 PM.*
>
> *Nor is Captain Matheson so influenced…*
>
> *All of the jurors living make the same plea…*
>
> *Nor could Bishop Parsons of the Episcopal Church, Archbishop Hanna of the Roman Catholic Church, nor David Starr Jordan, have been so influenced.*
>
> *I never had any personal interest in Mooney either before or after the bomb explosion. I knew him casually as a labor man, but had not espoused any of his causes or regarded him as in any way a potential labor leader.*
>
> *All through the trial I believed him guilty, and instructed the writers who reported the bomb trials to not color the news at all—to merely print the evidence as it was given, drawing no conclusions whatever.*

Then Andrew Furuseth, a labor man in whom I have the utmost faith, came from the East, called upon me and told me he had seen some letters which convinced him there was something rotten in the Mooney case. These letters, according to Furuseth, were written by Oxman to an old pal of his, a man named Rigall, a rather disreputable character living in…Illinois.

In a few days the letters came and were shown to me. They seemed authentic but I did not publish them until I had been informed on good authority that Oxman admitted having written them. It was then that I first became interested in the Mooney case. I saw clearly that the prosecution would not have permitted such perjured testimony as Oxman was willing to introduce if they had anything but a framed case.

Since that time I have continued the investigation of all the other witnesses and the result is that at the present time there is no evidence at all that either Mooney or Billings had anything to do with the crime…

It is not my interest in Mooney that has kept me at work on this case through so many years. It has rather been the desire to save the state of California from persisting in such a flagrant piece of injustice as has been done in this case…

You informed Mr. Rowell that you would not pardon these men, but that their procedure should be first through parole. You also say that even parole should not be invoked except at the proper time, whatever that may mean. I am sure the Prison Board will not parole these men unless they know you are favorable to it…

I wrote you a letter last April setting forth the high points of this case and have received no answer from you. I believe your secretary acknowledged receipt of the letter. That was all. I am enclosing you a copy of that letter fearing that possibly you have been too busy to read it.

In January 1928, Older had a conference with Young, after which he wrote to Billings that he had no hope that the governor would pardon either him or Mooney. The defense had been joined by the prominent New York lawyer Frank Walsh, who had been chairman of the Federal Commission on Industrial Relations; the Mooney case, he said, made his blood boil. After several months' delay, a conference with the governor was arranged at which Older, Walsh, Andrew Furuseth, Judge Griffin, District Attorney Brady, Mooney's juror MacNevin, political writer Franklin Hichborn and several labor leaders appealed for Mooney's freedom. Frank Walsh, said Older, "made a very powerful and convincing presentation of the case," in which he stripped the prosecution of any case at all and demonstrated that Billings and Mooney "could not be arrested for anything." Judge Griffin said that Governor Richardson did not pardon either man because "he was too cowardly to do it. It takes courage to pardon them." Young took exception, asking Griffin if he was calling him a coward. Griffin said he wasn't. Again Older was discouraged. He wrote to Billings, "I don't think [Young] wants to pardon you and Mooney…unless there is a great deal of agitation and pressure."

In 1929, Older enjoyed a sort of professional triumph. When he left the *Bulletin* in 1918, the exodus of staff was joined by an exodus of subscribers. Within a few years, according to Older's biographer, Evelyn Wells, the paper lost $125,000 in one month. Crothers and Pickering sold out their interest, and the next owner subsequently sold what was left of the *Bulletin*—practically nothing—to Hearst for $1 million. (Hearst was reportedly so angry at having paid so much for a worthless property that he fired the executive responsible.) The *Call and Post*, under Older's management, merged with the old *Bulletin* to form the *Call-Bulletin*. Older was never so busy with Billings-Mooney that he couldn't innovate journalistically: longtime San Franciscans will remember that the *Call-Bulletin* was printed on pale salmon-colored paper, which made it stand out on newsstands.

Late in 1929, after purportedly studying the transcripts of Mooney's trial, Young "discovered" the Billings case, which he said was parallel to Mooney's, and suggested that Billings also apply for a pardon. That might have seemed fair, but it was really a way out for Young: Billings had been convicted in 1916 of transporting dynamite, as well as for the Preparedness Day bombing, and under an 1879 law, a prisoner with two felony convictions could be pardoned only at the recommendation of a majority of the justices of the California Supreme Court. Young had to know that the justices were unsympathetic.

Billings had made a remarkable adjustment to prison, particularly Folsom, in the Sierra foothills above Sacramento. He still looked little older than an adolescent; he had studied law, Latin, English, Spanish and Russian; and he had become an accomplished chess player by correspondence. In February 1928, he wrote to Fremont Older:

> *I have been wrongly accused, unjustly imprisoned and generally unfairly taken advantage of yet I do not complain—nor am I vindictive or vengeful. I ask only that I be restored to my liberty in a fair and honest manner and if this can be done I shall even be duly grateful to those to whom I may be beholden for it although everyone must realize that this much at least, is truthfully my due.*

Furthermore—I do not feel that I am, or have ever been—a martyr… I'm just "the goat." An unfortunate victim of circumstances and my own folly. I don't consider that anyone else is responsible for my plight either. Whatever other people did in this case—whether they were witnesses or prosecutors or judges—was no doubt done in the light of "duty"—they followed the dictates of their own conscience and I have enough faith in the law of compensation to believe that their own consciences will punish them if they have done wrong. If I have ever done any wrong I think that I have by now suffered sufficiently for it. More than eleven years in prison should atone for almost any crime but murder and I am certain that that at least is one crime of which I am totally innocent.

Since I have been in prison I have formulated a philosophy and a code of morals for the future which is based entirely upon the code of Justinian, Emperor of Rome, who said "Live honestly, hurt nobody and render to every man his just due. This being thoroughly understood, do as you please." This is the code I hope to live up to after I am released and if I succeed in following it but a little of the way I shall feel that I am not much less respectable than other men.

Yes, I think that if my case could be presented to the governor in the proper manner he would be very willing to commute my sentence to time served. At least, I insist upon making the attempt. One thing at least that my incarceration has done to me—it has made me "hard-headed"—I am no longer easily led nor easily swayed from the ways which I have set myself to go—and I am patient—very, very patient.

Billings applied for a pardon. The California State Supreme Court's hearings on it went on until Thursday, July 3, 1930, the day before Billings's birthday. Predictably, the judges voted six to one against pardon. While the Edeaus' testimony had been discredited, the judges said that Estelle Smith's and John McDonald's still stood. The judges conveniently overlooked the fact that Smith's and McDonald's testimonies contradicted each other, putting Billings in two different places about a mile apart at the same time. The court concluded, in reasoning that was not only extralegal but also bordered on the fantastic:

It is an almost irresistible conclusion that if Warren K. Billings did not himself prepare and plant the deadly time bomb of the Preparedness Day disaster, he and his intimate associates and co-defendant Mooney know and have always…known who did…and the deadly purpose for which it was prepared and planted.

Yet there has never come from the lips of either of these defendants, or from the inner circle of their associates, the slightest tangible hint or aid to the public officials or to anyone else which might lead to a discovery of the real perpetrators…if these two defendants were not the guilty ones.

Young received the judges' decision the same Thursday, July 3. On Monday, July 5, he announced his decision not to pardon Warren Billings. It was a shock to Older, who up until the day before the decision had believed that the governor would pardon both Billings and Mooney. Young, however, added one qualification: John McDonald had not testified at Billings's application for pardon. Suggesting a possible reopening of the case, Young "would respectfully suggest to the…supreme court, should John McDonald, or any other material witness who has repudiated his former testimony, appear before them for the purpose of proving such repudiations as trustworthy…it may be only just and right to consider the propriety of giving hear to such witnesses in the case of Billings." It was another obvious out for Young. The *Call-Bulletin* reported that McDonald had dropped out of sight in 1923. He was unwell then "and is believed to be dead."

To the amazement of all concerned, McDonald was not dead! After the Scripps-Howard newspaper chain posted his picture along with a reward notice, a reporter spotted him in a Baltimore jail drunk tank on July 12. Released, he said that he would indeed repudiate the testimony he gave in the trials of Billings and Mooney and began the trip west, accompanied by attorneys Charles Ruzicka and Hilary Gans. Young, with his usual gift for delay, said that he would like a public hearing to be held after the state primary elections on August 26. The defense protested that McDonald, obviously very unwell, might not live until then, particularly after the stress of a transcontinental train trip. On July 15, Young backtracked, proposing that McDonald be given a joint hearing before himself, the State Supreme Court and the State Pardon Board in a general reopening of the Billings-Mooney case "very promptly after McDonald gets to California."

On Monday, July 21, 1930, the newspapers reported that the State Supreme Court would reconsider Billings's application for a pardon. The hearings began on Tuesday, July 29. The procedure was unprecedented, with a quasi-prosecution and quasi-defense. Fickert, now practicing in Los Angeles, appeared for the "prosecution," assisted by former aides Fred Berry and Louis Ferrari. "Defense" included the attorneys who had accompanied McDonald from Baltimore, Edwin McKenzie for Billings and Frank P. Walsh for Mooney. Estelle Smith, McDonald and other figures, including Cunha, testified.

An old, sick McDonald, *right*, returns to San Francisco accompanied by lawyer Charles Ruzicka. *San Francisco Public Library History Room.*

As this was a hearing and not a court session, the ordinary rules of procedure did not apply. Billings and Mooney did not attend. The justices, with one exception, conducted themselves in a way that shocked even veteran reporters. Justice John Preston did most of the questioning. Harping on Billings's alleged radicalism, Preston led Cunha into stating that Mooney should be hanged for "aiding and abetting," whether Billings and Mooney were at Steuart Street or not.

Under Preston's questioning, John McDonald broke down repeatedly and had to be revived with water. "It was all a pack of lies," he sobbed about his testimony at Billings's and Mooney's trials. He had come to California because of "qualms of conscience," and he had "no fear of telling the truth and is allied with no influences which would deflect him from the truth."

"Have you any realization of the position you appear in at this time?" Preston asked.

"Yes."

"Have you any evidence to give us to show us that you are telling the truth now rather than then?"

"Only your own judgment," answered McDonald. "I was taken to the district attorney's office and forced to tell a false story. It seemed as if I was in the clutches of Charles Fickert, and couldn't get out. He gave me twenty dollars on election day, and then he set me up on a ranch near Tracy owned by a man named Drew."

"Did you receive wages for your work on this ranch?"

"Yes. I got wages but I didn't do any work."

Estelle Smith rambled almost incoherently, unable to stop. She spoke of Fremont Older's influence on her, which gave Preston an opening he obviously wanted. Older was called to testify. As author Lillian Symes said, the justices had not forgiven nor forgotten Older's exposure in 1918 of Justice Henshaw's taking a $400,000 bribe from the heirs of James Fair to change his vote in their favor. Preston now implied an illicit relationship between Estelle Smith and Older, intimating that he had plied her with food, wine and jewelry. In fact, Older had treated Smith to meals while gaining her confidence. The jewelry was innocent. A friend of Cora's had sent her some strings of Japanese artificial pearls. Not caring for them, Cora told Fremont to take them to his office and let any staff who wanted them have them. He also let Estelle Smith have one. Cora had wanted to testify in corroboration, but Fremont, perhaps overly protective, would not let her be subject to Preston's interrogation.

Older testified on Monday, August 18. Asked how he came to be connected with the case, he said that he was not really interested until he saw the Oxman letters. "Then I became convinced that Mooney and Billings were innocent. I was convinced that if the prosecution had any real case they would not have allowed Oxman to take the stand." About Estelle Smith, he said at first that he disliked the defense's attacking her character. "It occurred to me that if I could meet her and obtain her friendship I might interest her in modifying the statements she had made under oath identifying Billings as being present at 721 Market Street." Preston continued on the subject of Estelle Smith.

"You said you explained to Estelle Smith your attitude toward life and those who are under a cloud—what did you mean?"

"I mean that I don't judge anybody, separate the so-called good people from the so-called bad people. My ideas are the same as those of Christ in the sermon on the mount."

Evidently distrusting the source of Older's philosophy, Preston asked, "Of what descent are you? Are you native born?"

"I am native born—of English descent on both sides."

"How long have you held these ideas?"

"I believe I acquired them during the graft prosecution."

"You did not get them from your forebears, then?"

"No. I developed my ideas myself. I told Estelle that I had no feeling of superiority—that we are all just human beings struggling along as best we can."

Turning to Smith's original testimony in Billings's trial that she saw Billings on the roof of 721 Market Street with a heavy camera case—not a suitcase like the one at Steuart Street—and that she had wiped perspiration from his forehead with a wet towel, Preston, asked "Well, do you believe she saw a man on the roof?"

"Probably," Older answered.

"Was this man sick and did she wipe his forehead with a towel?"

"I have no means of knowing."

"Well, I ask you to judge your very dear friend Estelle."

The tone of Preston's question brought Billings's attorney, McKenzie, to his feet immediately: "I resent that imputation."

"Oh, well, let it go," murmured Older.

"You know I only use such words for euphony," Preston smiled.

"Then I ask that you insert an apology," McKenzie insisted.

The next day, Tuesday, August 19, Preston continued on a line of questioning ranging through philosophy, religion and pearl jewelry. Because of Older's attitude toward human frailty—which included judges—he practically suggested that Older bore some responsibility for the bombing. Older bore it all calmly.

In late August, the judges went to Folsom Prison to interrogate Billings. During the San Francisco hearings, McDonald's original description, witnessed by two police officers, of the two men at Steuart Street was

Fremont Older, circa 1930, about the time of Billings's pardon application. *San Francisco Public Library History Room.*

produced, but it had no effect. Preston and other judges pursued the same type of questioning of Billings that they had of Older: his background, his beliefs and his activities. Billings had become quite candid, including his spraying paint remover on automobiles the day of the Preparedness parade. His candor was used against him.

Late in November, the judges, to no one's surprise, again voted six to one against Billings's pardon. The dissenter was William Langdon, the former San Francisco district attorney who surprised Fremont Older in 1906 by vowing to prosecute any man who broke the law—even Abraham Ruef, who had put him on the Union Labor Party ticket. Langdon's career was characterized by honesty and conscientiousness. His dissent was eloquent and convincing:

> *Considered either as an argument of an advocate or as a judicial review of the evidence, the consolidated majority report of the Supreme Court is unsound and indefensible. It is unsound because its conclusions are not founded upon established facts. Suspicions, conjectures, unwarranted inferences, irreconcilable inconsistencies, and admitted perjuries are treated as facts. It is indefensible because it appeals to passion and prejudice.*
>
> *One-fourth of the report is devoted to anarchistic propaganda and the bad character of the petitioner. The Trial Court properly held these matters were not admissible. It is manifestly improper to inject them into this inquiry…*
>
> *The requirement of the majority that the petitioner prove his innocence, either by establishing an alibi or by identifying the perpetrator of the crime, is unreasonable and unwarranted. A perfectly innocent person may be unable to prove an alibi. And it is preposterous to demand of the accused that he place his finger upon the real culprit in order to exculpate himself.*

> *Although Billings had presented an alibi, it is unnecessary for us to consider it. When the chain of proof is destroyed he needs none.*
>
> *I do not know whether Billings is guilty or innocent of the crime. I do know that there has been a failure of proof to such an extent that there is now not even a semblance of a case against him. Upon the record now before us a recommendation for executive clemency cannot justly be withheld.*

The August gubernatorial primary elections, which Young had wanted to use to delay the rehearing of Billings's application, were a surprise. Running again for governor, Mayor James ("Sunny Jim") Rolph defeated Young by twenty thousand votes. Like Stephens and Richardson before him, Young was a lame duck and could have pardoned Mooney but did not. Sunny Jim Rolph was elected in November. His inauguration was a three-day gala, but his inaugural address was interrupted when a fifty-foot banner proclaiming

Demonstration for Mooney in Union Square, New York City, October 10, 1931. *San Francisco Public Library History Room.*

Mooney's innocence was unfurled from the state capitol dome, and during the inaugural parade, an ancient hearse suddenly displayed signs reading "Free Tom Mooney" as it passed the reviewing stand. Rolph characteristically promised to "fill California with smiles," but as the Depression gripped the United States and the state of California, it was apparent that Rolph was unable to deal with it.

Rolph, who had stormed out of Fremont Older's office after hearing Officer Draper Hand's revelations, was reluctant to do anything about something so bitterly divisive. Approached by members of a Mooney defense committee, he professed to be too busy with matters of state and then suddenly burst out with how he had been leading the Preparedness Day parade when the bomb went off and saw the dead victims at Steuart Street—which was true but irrelevant. The defense kept the pressure up on Rolph, although without much hope. James "Jimmy" Walker, the flamboyant Tammany Hall Democratic mayor of New York who had learned about Mooney from Frank Walsh, made a special trip to San Francisco on Mooney's behalf, supposedly because of a telegram from Tom's mother, Mary:

> *Dear Mayor Walker: I am eighty years old. Afraid I am breaking down at last. They want to take me to a hospital tomorrow. In the name of God and His Blessed Mother won't you come out to help my boy. It is my last chance to put my arms around him before I meet my God. He has been a good son to me. If you do this for Tom you will have my prayers as long as you live.*

In November 1931, Walker, Frank Walsh, New York lawyer Aaron Sapiro (a San Francisco native whose Lowell High English teacher was C.C. Young) and Ed Nockels of the Chicago Federation of Labor went to San Francisco. Once again, a defendant had applied for pardon to a governor—Rolph—and a hearing was to be held before the California Supreme Court in San Francisco in December. In San Francisco, Walker met with Rolph and Mayor Angelo Rossi, saw Mary Mooney and Tom's sister, Anna, in their Clipper Street home in the Mission District and saw Tom in San Quentin. He did not see Billings. The Supreme Court heard Walsh, Sapiro and Walker. Rolph said that he would confer with his legal advisors and render a decision, probably after three months. Walker conferred more national attention on Mooney, but his motives, and effect on the case, were debatable: Walker's administration was under investigation by New York State's Seabury Commission, and Governor Franklin D. Roosevelt had summoned Walker to Albany to give him a chance to resign, which he finally did late in 1932. San Francisco newspapers told Walker to mind his own business.

In April 1932, Rolph denied the defense's petition for a pardon, saying that he was convinced of Mooney's guilt. His legal advisors were Lewis Byington, who had been district attorney when Abraham Ruef controlled San Francisco, and Matt Sullivan, who had briefly been a justice of the California State Supreme Court and who had defended Fremont Older in a libel charge brought by multimillionaire landowner Lloyd Tevis—another break with a former ally of Older's over Billings-Mooney. Rolph cited an eighty-eight-page report by Sullivan, most of which was an attack on Mooney and his radicalism and which concluded that Mooney was guilty because he was convicted. Sullivan cited Judge Dunne as an authority and dismissed Griffin's "fulminations." But Dunne was *Billings's* judge. Sullivan's report prompted a scathing reply from Aaron Sapiro:

> *Why, Judge Sullivan, do you give ear only to Judge Dunne, who did not sit in the Mooney case, and close your ears to Judge Griffin, who was the presiding judge?...*
>
> *Does the fact that Judge Dunne sides with your preconception and prejudices make him right?*
>
> *Does the fact that Judge Griffin boldly and frankly asserts that Mooney's conviction was improper cause you to brush his words aside as "the fulminations of a much younger judge?" And when did old age become synonymous with a clear mind and the ability to render justice? Do you refer to it to justify yourself, Judge Sullivan?* [Sullivan was seventy-five.]

Sullivan's report called Oxman's testimony "not indispensable," but several jurors, including Foreman MacNevin, and Judge Griffin said it *was* indispensable to the prosecution's case. And if Oxman's testimony was not indispensable, whose was? Certainly not that of the Edeaus or Estelle Smith, who had Billings and Mooney at 721 Market. That left only McDonald, whose 1916 affidavit, now revealed, described two men similar to those seen by other witnesses who could not have been Billings or Mooney. The reply charged that Sullivan's report was "an amazing document, coming from a lawyer and former judge," one that "bristles with evasions, misrepresentations, insinuations, cheap emotionalism and bitter prejudice," and it charged Sullivan with keeping an innocent man in prison because of "your hatred of his views and activities in the cause of organized labor." The reply was signed by Roger Baldwin of the American Civil Liberties Union; educator John Dewey; journalists Fremont Older, Lemuel Parton, Oswald Garrison Villard and Ernest Jerome ; and Rabbi Stephen S. Wise, among others.

Sullivan's attitude was demonstrative of a perverse reinforcing relationship that had developed through the years of Billings-Mooney. A governor like Young said that the courts had convicted them, so he could not interfere without their approval. The courts, for their part, said that the defendants' only recourse was to the governor.

The Billings-Mooney case produced a huge amount of written and visual material. A film in Mooney's defense appeared as early as 1917, and by 1932, there were so many books, magazine and newspaper articles, editorials and legal documents that one could make a career of reading them. In May 1931, *Harper's Magazine* published the aptly titled "Our American Dreyfus Case," by journalist Lillian Symes, who chided citizens of the United States and particularly of California for lacking social idealism and indignation "in the face of palpable injustice and stupidity." While admitting that Rolph might pardon Billings and Mooney—a possibility she thought remote—Symes deplored their incarceration, which continued only because they had been unpopular:

> *California, like all our states, abounds with persons who feel that anyone suspected of subversive opinions regarding this best of all possible worlds is better off in jail. But few Californians, except the more simple-minded readers of the San Francisco* Chronicle *and the Los Angeles* Times *believe for a moment that Thomas J. Mooney and Warren K. Billings are guilty of the crime of which they were convicted.*

Symes's article quoted three federal reports: President Wilson's 1917 Mediation Commission Report, the 1918 Densmore Report and a recent one known as the Wickersham Report, after George Wickersham, attorney general under President Taft and chairman of a federal commission assigned to investigate lawless and unfair police practices. The commission did not publish the report officially, as it believed that it was not empowered to investigate specific cases, but Roger Baldwin of the American Civil Liberties Union had it published privately. The 243-page report, written by three attorneys—Zechariah Chafee Jr. of the Harvard law faculty and New York lawyers and partners Walter Pollak and Carl Stern—examined the Billings-Mooney case in detail and concluded:

> *There was never any scientific attempt made by either the police or the prosecution to discover the perpetrators of the crime. The investigation was in reality turned over to a private detective, who used his position to cause the arrest of the defendants. The police investigation was reduced to a hunt for evidence…*
>
> *There were flagrant violations of the statutory law of California by…* [police and prosecution] *in the manner in which the defendants were arrested and held incommunicado, and in the subsequent searches of their homes…*
>
> *After the arrest of the defendants, witnesses were brought to the jails to "identify" them, and their "identifications" were accepted by the police and the prosecution* [although] *these witnesses were never required to pick the defendants out of a line-up…*
>
> *Witnesses were produced at the trials with information in the hands of the prosecution that seriously challenged the credibility of the witnesses, but this information was deliberately concealed.*
>
> *Witnesses were permitted to testify at the trials, despite such knowledge in the possession of the prosecution of prior contradictory stories told by these witnesses, as to make their mere production a vouching for perjured testimony.*

Symes buttressed her article with appendices. One was a letter from Matheson to Mooney supporting Mooney's pardon application; Matheson called Oxman a "romancer" who should have been convicted of suborning perjury. Another quoted Judge Griffin saying that if he were governor, his first act would be to pardon Mooney: "The Mooney case is one of the dirtiest jobs ever put over and I resent the fact that my court was used for such a contemptible piece of work."

In 1931, Fremont Older's *Call-Bulletin* serialized a second autobiographical work by Older, *Growing Up*. Older had gone to work at age ten and had sought relief from his Dickensian boyhood in literature and the stage. He remembered Victorian melodramas that always ended happily, with the hero marrying the girl. Of the Billings-Mooney case, he wrote, "Now if this drama had been prepared for the stage, the curtain would have dropped, with Mooney released, and Oxman, who tried to lie his life away, being handcuffed and led off stage by the police. But unfortunately, this is real life and not stage fiction. Oxman, the perjurer, retired to his home in Oregon to spend his life in comfort and Mooney remained in prison."

In fact, the Mooney case did make the stage. In 1931, movie star Jean Harlow's husband, Paul Bern, produced a Broadway play, *Precedent*,

Still showing the old fire at age seventy-six, Fremont Older addresses the American Civil Liberties Union on Billings-Mooney in 1932. *Bancroft Library.*

written by I.J. Golden. The protagonist, Delaney (Mooney), is convicted of a bombing on perjured testimony. In the last act, he is in San Quentin, while a crusading newspaper editor named Fremont tries to get him out. *New York Times* drama critic Brooks Atkinson reviewed *Precedent* favorably:

> *Being frankly a propaganda play, "Precedent," which was acted at the old Provincetown last evening, makes no pretensions toward being sound drama. But the astonishing thing about this exposition of the cause célèbre*

> *of Tom Mooney is the strong appeal it has in the theatre…It is acted with fervent sincerity by an excellent troupe of performers…*
>
> *In retelling, for the defense, the story of the conviction of Tom Mooney and the repeated attempts to secure a pardon, Mr. Golden is as temperate as he is earnest. Although he invents names for his characters, you will recognize among his people Judge Griffin, who presided at the trial* [fifteen] *years ago; Fremont Older, who has worked unselfishly to have Mooney pardoned; District Attorney Fickert, who won the State's case, and two of the chief witnesses for the prosecution, Estelle Smith and F.C. Oxman…*
>
> *Friends of Tom Mooney will rejoice to have his case told so crisply and vividly.*

If Rolph thought that refusing to pardon Mooney would end the agitation, he was in for a shock. As Rolph and U.S. Vice President Charles Curtis presided at the closing ceremonies of the 1932 Los Angeles Olympic Games, four young men and two young women in track gear jumped from the Coliseum stands, and circled the field wearing "Free Tom Mooney" badges big enough to be read by the crowd. In the confusion, two other men ran onto the field and displayed a banner similarly emblazoned. Rolph froze. Police arrested the disturbers and escorted them from the stadium, and they were given six-month sentences. Nationally and worldwide, an extraordinary roster of prominent men and women endorsed or actively supported Mooney's campaign: writers Theodore Dreiser, Lincoln Steffens, H.G. Wells, Fannie Hurst, Carl Sandburg, Edna Ferber, William Allen White, George Bernard Shaw and Sinclair Lewis; violinist Yehudi Menuhin; Hollywood figures Fredric March, James Cagney and Boris Karloff; several United States senators; both houses of the state legislature of Wisconsin; the House of Representatives of the State of Minnesota; the entire law faculty of the University of Oregon; and Albert Einstein.

Tom's mother, Mary, traveled throughout the United States and Europe on Tom's behalf. Mary was a pitiful figure, over eighty years old and unwell, neither educated nor articulate, with a thick brogue from her Irish upbringing. But her artlessness, which prevented her from being able to finish a speech to crowds—members of defense committees had to read them for her—touched her listeners. She made two trips in 1932, going to Europe on the second, with stops in the Soviet Union, Holland, France, Germany, England and Ireland (her first visit since emigrating). Back in the United States, Mary went to Albany, New York, and on December 30, 1932, she met the most prominent man of all: president-elect Franklin Delano

Roosevelt. FDR was on the point of leaving the governorship and was, of course, quite busy, but he took time to accept a letter from Mary personally. Mary's letter referred to a man named Callicotte, who confessed to planting the Preparedness Day bomb (Callicotte's "confession" was fake). Roosevelt promised to write Rolph as a citizen and did:

> *Mrs. Mary Mooney came to see me yesterday and left me with the enclosed letter. I told her that in my capacity as governor I could not interfere in any way with the functions of an executive of another state. However, as I am going out of my office today I told her that I would send you her letter in my private capacity, and that I would do so solely on the ground that her letter represents that additional evidence has been discovered since your recent action—more especially a confession which she says was made by one Callicotte.*

Rolph took no further action. As 1932 ended, Billings and Mooney had been in jail for sixteen and a half years.

The defense had held open the option of having Mooney tried on the one remaining indictment that Judge Griffin had refused to let be dismissed. Acquittal would not free Billings or Mooney, but it would legally demonstrate the lack of a case on the original charge and would increase pressure on Rolph. District Attorney Brady, however, although supposedly sympathetic to the defense, indicated that he would move for a directed acquittal, arguing that a trial would be an expensive farce: Oxman had died in 1931, so there was no material witness. The defense protested that the Edeaus, McDonald and Estelle Smith were available. It was a strange spectacle—the Mooney side demanding a trial and the district attorney demanding acquittal without one. Brady left the case to his assistant, William Murphy.

Proceedings were scheduled before Judge Louis Ward for the end of April 1933. In view of Brady's reluctance, Ward asked California attorney general Ulysses Webb to appoint a special prosecutor, but Webb refused. On the first day, mobs surround the Hall of Justice on Kearny Street, and shouts of "Free Tom Mooney" penetrated the courtroom. Ward postponed the trial until the end of May. This time, police cleared the area, and there were no demonstrations. Writer Miriam Allen deFord, in an article for *The Nation*, observed two sets of actors in court: the new figures of the present trial (Judge Ward; Assistant District Attorney Murphy, who seemed embarrassed; the younger defense attorneys) and the "ghosts," physically present or not (Fickert, Oxman, McDonald, Estelle Smith, the Edeaus, former police sergeant Goff, Tom's family—mother Mary, sister Anna, brother John and Rena, "a tragic, harrowed figure, a tear-wasted caricature of the blooming young woman of 1916"—and Tom Mooney himself).

After a lengthy examination of prospective jurors, the jury was sworn. The proceedings moved to their foregone conclusion when Murphy declared that "the evidence in this case is insufficient...The defendant is entitled to rest behind a plea of not guilty and the presumption of innocence." Mooney, acting as his own counsel—always a mistake—repeated his demand for a trial: "You say the evidence is insufficient to convict me. Four governors, the prison pardon board, and the Supreme Court have held that same evidence sufficient to hold me in San Quentin. If it is sufficient for that, it is sufficient to place before a jury." Murphy seemed to hesitate. Then, repeating the old argument that the case rested before the governor, he "got himself through his distasteful job," as deFord wrote. The jury acquitted without leaving the courtroom.

About the same time, the defense produced a fifteen-minute movie, *The Strange Case of Tom Mooney*, that included films of the Preparedness Day parade, the carnage at Steuart Street, Mooney's trial and multiple stills of Swanson, Oxman, McDonald, the Edeaus and others. It ended with a head-and-shoulders shot of Mooney demanding that the district attorney present all the evidence. As the camera moves in for a close-up, Mooney thanks his friends throughout the world for their loyal support; his voice breaking with emotion, Mooney expresses his hope that some day they will meet under more auspicious circumstances.

The publicity campaign was a success: in 1935, journalist John Barry of the *San Francisco News* would note that in Europe, the four most famous Americans were Franklin D. Roosevelt, Charles A Lindbergh, Henry Ford and Tom Mooney. Legally, however, appeal after appeal to the governors, the courts of California and the courts of San Francisco had failed. Billings and Mooney had been in jail for more than nineteen years.

The Newsboy Who Became a Lawyer

There was one last legal maneuver, apparently first suggested by Billings himself. As early as the 1920s, Billings reasoned that the convictions were violations of the Fifth and Fourteenth Amendments to the United States Constitution. The Fifth stated that no person shall "be deprived of life, liberty, or property, without due process of law." The Fourteenth extended the protection: no *state* shall "deprive any person of life, liberty, or property, without due process of law." Perjured testimony was clearly not due process of law, as Billings saw it, therefore he and Mooney were entitled to release under habeas corpus, the ancient common-law writ, codified in England in 1679, directing law officers to bring persons held unjustly by a lower court before a higher one.

At the time, Billings's idea seemed far-fetched. Federal courts did not apply the United States Constitution that way. Even Clarence Darrow, lawyers for the American Civil Liberties Union and Frank Walsh thought that nothing would come of it. Billings reacted with uncharacteristic anger: "All I have to say in rebuttal is that if there *is* no legal remedy for this judicial error then this is *one hell of a country to live in*!" By 1934, however, federal courts had applied the writ as Billings suggested. Frank Walsh and Washington, D.C. lawyer John Finerty were planning an appeal based on the Wickersham Report's charge that Fickert had knowingly suppressed evidence that would have resulted in Mooney's acquittal. As Fickert was an agent of the State of California, California had denied due process.

Habeas corpus proceedings would be long and complicated, and Walsh and Finerty came to San Francisco to consult a local counsel about submitting the case to Federal District Court. Fremont Older had arranged for a local lawyer named John Taafe to meet Walsh and Finerty in his office, but Taafe had gotten an offer from two Reno gamblers who had been arrested for wire fraud in New York to be their lawyer, and while Walsh and Finerty were taking a train west, Taafe was on one going east. In Older's office, Walsh and Finerty asked Older if he had any ideas for another lawyer. Older hadn't, but he knew John Denman, a prominent labor lawyer. Denman couldn't suggest anyone to Walsh and Finerty on the spur of the moment and asked a young lawyer named Lyman Henry in his office if he knew someone his own age who might be interested in taking the Mooney case to federal court.

Lyman Henry suggested his acquaintance George T. Davis, who, in a fantastic coincidence, was the newsboy George T. Davis hawking the *Chronicle* in front of the Palace Hotel on Preparedness Day when the bomb exploded; who ran with his newspapers to Steuart Street and saw the dead and wounded; who saw Sergeant Bunner wash the evidence down the sewer with a fire hose; who heard Matheson ask Bunner what he was doing; and who saw Fickert and chamber of commerce official Colburn pound the bomb site with a sledgehammer. Davis had worked his way through high school, the University of California–Berkeley and the law school there; had worked briefly in District Attorney Brady's office; and had gone into partnership with a classmate. Although just twenty-seven, he already had a considerable local reputation as a criminal lawyer, having won all but one of his cases, often with unorthodox but effective methods. He had one rule for himself: never turn down a case involving the death penalty.

Henry and Davis had discussed the Mooney case occasionally, but when Henry called Davis and said that Walsh and Finerty wanted to talk to him about it, he was too surprised to answer. Henry gave him a day to think about it, and Davis weighed the pros and cons. To the business community, Mooney was anathema, someone it wanted to get rid of on any excuse. To many labor men, Mooney was a hero. Davis had grown up South of Market and had heard about Mooney, and probably Billings, his whole life. It seemed that there was no one who could read who *hadn't* heard about the case, in California, the United States and the world, and Davis enjoyed publicity.

Davis's partner, Eli Freed, was opposed. Freed was starting as a business lawyer, making contacts with the right people, and told Davis that they would always be friends but that their partnership would be dissolved if Davis represented Mooney: "You've got to remember that there are people in San Francisco who wouldn't want to even be on the same side of the street with you if they knew that you were Mooney's lawyer." The partnership was dissolved, and Davis never entered another one, which was good for a maverick like him.

Davis called Lyman Henry to tell him that he was interested, and he met Walsh and Finerty for lunch. Davis said that he had always believed Mooney innocent and that there had been a denial of due process. Walsh and Finerty were impressed, telling Davis that their minds had been moving in that very direction. They outlined their plans for an appeal to the federal courts based on Mooney's conviction on perjured testimony. This didn't just excite Davis; it "lit a fire under me." As he learned the details of the case, he became horrified that such things could have happened under any legal system. A man had been tried and convicted of murder; it was demonstrated unequivocally that every witness against him had committed perjury, and he had no legal remedy? Davis couldn't believe it.

Davis was devoted to the law, and his energy seemed inexhaustible. He threw himself into preparing the case, and the petition reached the Federal District Court early in 1934. In May, the court predictably decided that

> [t]*he exceptional cases in which a federal court or judge may sometimes appropriately interfere by habeas corpus in advance of final action by the authorities of the state are those of great urgency, that require to be promptly disposed of... The present case is not within any of the exceptions recognized in our former decisions. Petition denied.*

Davis appealed to the United States Circuit Court, to similar results:

> *The fact that petitioner did not learn of the alleged perjured testimony and of the alleged misconduct of the district attorney who prosecuted him until it was too late to assign same as grounds for a new trial is indeed unfortunate. The petition is denied.*

The next, and last, appeal was to the Supreme Court of the United States.

In California, 1934 was a turbulent year that those who lived through it never forgot. Rolph's administration was incompetent, and his expenses were under investigation. Rolph himself was a sick man, and on June 2, he suddenly died. His body was returned to his beloved San Francisco and lay in state below the dome of the magnificent city hall that he dedicated as mayor. He was succeeded by Lieutenant Governor Frank Merriam, a colorless conservative Republican who said that he would make no decision on Billings-

Mooney unless and until elected in November. Merriam's Democratic opponent was the novelist Upton Sinclair, who had first attracted national attention with *The Jungle*, the exposé of Chicago meat processing that made readers literally sick. In 1920, Fremont Older had suggested that Sinclair write a novel about the Mooney case, and the result was *100%: The Story of a Patriot*—not a great seller. Sinclair's gubernatorial campaign slogan was "End Poverty in California" ("EPIC"), which Sinclair, who had previously run as a socialist, proposed to do with untested schemes involving "production for use" and heavy taxes on production for profit. In 1933, Sinclair publicized his proposals in *I, Governor of California and How I Ended Poverty: A True Story of the Future.* In Sinclair's novel, his first act as governor was to call the San Quentin warden and order Tom Mooney's release on a pardon.

The Market Street fault soon shook again. In the 1920s, San Francisco employers, exploiting the anti-labor feeling generated by the Preparedness Day bomb and the Law and Order Committee, had formed the Industrial Association to finish off union labor. A company union ran hiring on the waterfront. The International Longshoremen's Association, under the leadership of thirty-three-year-old Australian immigrant Harry Bridges, demanded recognition and struck after the employers refused. The strike spread from San Diego to Seattle. In July, the Industrial Association brought in scab workers with police protection, and on July 5, "Bloody Thursday," the police fired first tear gas and then bullets. Two strikers were killed. Merriam called in the National Guard, and a four-day general strike followed. To Fremont Older and his allies, it must have seemed depressingly familiar—the old lines of battle redrawn, with violence and instability.

On Saturday, September 1, Mary Mooney saw Tom at San Quentin. Monday was Labor Day, and she was to appear in the parade. On Sunday, she was preparing dinner for Tom's brother, John, when a neighbor heard her moan and found her collapsed in a chair. She said, "Poor Tom," and died, aged eighty-six, in an ambulance. Tom was devastated. He asked to be allowed to attend her funeral, a request that Warden James Holohan relayed to Governor Merriam. Merriam refused on the grounds that only a pardon could allow Tom out. On Saturday the eighth, the funeral procession boarded a ferry to San Rafael and drove to San Quentin to give Tom a last look at Mary. Anna Mooney pleaded with Holohan, but he refused to let Tom out, and the procession returned to San Francisco. Mary's funeral was held in Civic Auditorium, with eulogies by Harry Bridges, John Mooney and others, and she was buried in San Rafael.

The 1934 gubernatorial contest between Sinclair and Merriam was dirty even by California standards. The public relations firm of Whitaker and Baxter smeared Sinclair, and the Hearst Corporation faked newsreels of hobos flooding California in anticipation of his election. Sinclair lacked funds, Franklin Roosevelt did not endorse him and a third candidate, Raymond Haight (grandson of Governor Henry Haight, after whom San Francisco's Haight Street is named), ran as a Progressive, splitting the non-Republican votes. On November 6, Merriam polled 1,138,620 votes, Sinclair 879,557 and Haight 302,519.

After the United States Circuit Court denied Mooney's appeal, Finerty filed a motion with the Supreme Court of the United States, supported by twelve volumes, for leave to file a petition for an original writ of habeas corpus. California attorney general Webb argued against, saying that no federal question was involved. On January 21, 1935, the Supreme Court ruled in favor of *Mooney v. Holohan* (294 U.S. 103), with Chief Justice Charles Evans Hughes writing the majority opinion:

> [I]*f a state has contrived a conviction through the pretense of a trial which in truth is but used as a means of depriving a defendant of liberty through a deliberate deception of court and jury by the presentation of testimony known to be perjured, such a contrivance by a state to procure the conviction and imprisonment of a defendant is as inconsistent with the rudimentary demands of justice as is the obtaining of a like result by intimidation. And the action of prosecuting officers on behalf of the state, like that of administrative officers in the execution of its laws, may constitute state action with the purview of the Fourteenth Amendment.*

It was a victory for the defense and for civil liberties, but it was only a start. The United States Supreme Court did not actually grant the motion for habeas corpus, as it was not satisfied that due process had been denied. In effect, the court said that if the prosecution had *knowingly* used perjured testimony to convict Mooney, California had to release him; if it didn't, the United States Supreme Court would. The case went back to the Supreme Court of California.

On August 30, 1934, Fremont Older turned seventy-eight. He had a heart condition and suffered a serious attack in September attributed to "heart asthma," a misnomer. His doctor advised him to stay in bed for two weeks doing nothing, not even reading. Older said that he would stay active and let the end come when it might. On Sunday, March 3, 1935, Fremont and Cora Older; their ward, Mary d'Antonio; and their chauffeur went to a camellia show in Sacramento. Older drafted a column on his favorite essayist, Montaigne, in the automobile as Cora and Mary went inside. When they returned, he said they were too early; he hadn't finished. Older drove down old Highway 99, and just outside Lodi, he began gasping for breath and then drooped over the wheel. At Vanosse Hospital in Stockton, he was pronounced dead of a heart attack. Billings and Mooney had lost their most relentless advocate. Older was interred at the Woodhills property the following Tuesday, March 5. For weeks, condolences came to Cora Older from all over the world.

On June 17, 1935, the California Supreme Court granted Mooney a hearing on the writ of habeas corpus. Davis heard that it was a ploy. The

Left to right: Warren Billings, Rena Mooney and Tom Mooney, together again for the first time in eighteen years at the habeas corpus hearing. *San Francisco Public Library History Room.*

Supreme Court would hold hearings, deny that due process had been denied and let itself off the hook by sending the case back to the back to the United States Supreme Court. The defense would just have to go along.

Davis asked the Supreme Court to conduct the hearing in San Francisco and to let Mooney and Billings be transferred from their respective prisons to the San Francisco County Jail in the sheriff's custody during the hearings. The newly elected sheriff was Dan Murphy, who had been president of the San Francisco Labor Council when Mooney was convicted. Convinced of Tom's innocence, he had been one of the first labor leaders to advocate his freedom, and he suggested a unique arrangement: Tom would promise not to try to escape or do anything that might embarrass Murphy; in return, he would be allowed to go anywhere within the city—and environs, as it turned out—under the nominal supervision of Deputy Archie McAllister, free in all but name. Tom promised, and Billings, when he arrived from Folsom, enjoyed the same freedom. The press knew about the arrangement but never revealed it.

The hearings would presumably take a few weeks. Instead, they went on sixteen months, until January 1937. The judges did not participate but rather appointed as referee a retired lawyer named Addison Shaw, a classmate of California chief justice William Waste. Shaw was also a former lawyer for PG&E, not a good omen for the defense, but Davis cultivated a good working relationship with him. That the hearings went on so long was not just because of the case's length and complexity: Shaw was paid fifty dollars per day—during the Depression, no less—and to get his fee, he needed only to gavel the day's session to order, even if he dismissed it five minutes later. The rest of the day, Davis worked, often with Tom's help. Billings acted as law clerk, and by his later recollection, he searched ninety-nine *thousand* pages of documents, to verify that this or that letter or transcript or whatever had been previously examined. Little was found that was new, but the defense discovered the transcript of Tom and Rena's interrogation in 1916 that Fickert said didn't exist.

Davis knew so much about the case by 1935 and was so able that he took complete charge of the defense. Walsh and Finerty remained mostly in the East. No one took a fee—Walsh advised Davis not to in a high-publicity case—although Finerty was reimbursed expenses. Assistant Attorney General William Cleary represented the state.

All the living principals from the beginning of the Billings-Mooney case appeared at the hearings, like the rerun of an old movie: the Mooneys; Billings; Nolan; Weinberg; McDonald; Hatcher; Officer Hand; Chief

Peterson; Officer Smith; Matheson; Goff; Bunner; defense lawyers McNutt, McKenzie and Lawlor; prosecutors Cunha, Brennan and Fickert; and Judge Griffin. Swanson, Older, Mary Mooney and Oxman were dead.

McDonald was dying at a hospital in Baltimore. On film, wearing a bathrobe, he testified that he saw two men at Steuart Street who were not Billings or Mooney. "Fickert and Cunha told me to say I saw an automobile down there," said McDonald, sipping from a water glass, "and I *didn't* see an automobile down there." He died soon after. Fickert was a wasted, alcoholic wreck who walked with difficulty. His wife had divorced him due to his drinking, gambling, abuse and failure to provide. Davis grilled Fickert relentlessly, suggesting that he and Swanson were responsible for the Preparedness Day bomb—Billings thought so—and brought up the searches and seizures without warrants, as well as the arrests without probable cause. Fickert said that the Epsom salts in Nolan's basement were bomb material.

The defense rented an apartment at 1924 Polk Street, where Billings, Mooney, Davis and other defense personnel met for lunch and to plan strategy. Word got around, and soon labor leaders, politicians and Hollywood celebrities were regular lunch guests. At Polk Street, Tom Mooney told George Davis something astounding: he had fallen in love with a young female member of his defense committee. Tom's "affair" may have been retaliatory. Rena, after the charges against her were dropped, may have been consorting, in Davis's words, with another man, and she had an alcohol problem. Davis told Tom to keep quiet, for if this got out, sympathy for him would evaporate and he would spend the rest of his life in jail.

Cleary, for the state, claimed no impropriety and no perjury, with or without the prosecution's knowledge. In January 1937, referee Shaw submitted a report that concluded the same, to no one's surprise. ("Simply awful," said Walsh.) The justices of the California Supreme Court heard arguments in April. Estolv Ward, the court clerk and a former son-in-law of Chief Justice William Waste, was in the office of the court secretary when Waste appeared with a stack of documents. He handed them to the secretary and told him to write the opinion, which would be *res adjudicata* ("the thing is already decided").

On October 29, 1937, the California State Supreme Court announced its decision *In the Matter of the Application of Thomas J. Mooney for a Writ of Habeas Corpus* (10 Cal.2d 1). By a vote of five to one, it denied the writ of habeas corpus. The decision was an amazing job of picking and choosing. Anything, however tenuous, that supported the prosecution's case was accepted. Anything, however convincing, that supported frame-up or perjury was rejected. The court waded through one impropriety, inconsistency or contradiction by the prosecution after another. Reaching all the way back to the original Mooney trial, the court accepted even Oxman's testimony and McDonald's trial testimony. McDonald's original description of the two men at Steuart Street wasn't accepted, but his not seeing the automobile that Oxman described didn't matter. "In our opinion," said the court, "the testimony of the two witnesses is not in irreconcilable conflict." The court also dismissed concerns about Oxman's letters to Rigall: "At the most, the letters indicate an attempted subornation of perjury." The court went on to stress who was and was not "reliable" or "unreliable." Oxman had only suborned perjury; that didn't make him "unreliable." The Hatchers' testimony was dismissed, as they must just have been cross with Oxman for not helping them after they had helped him.

The court resurrected the Edeaus. Oakland police chief Peterson and Officer William Smith, who had exposed them, were unreliable. Draper Hand was unreliable. McDonald's subsequent recantations were unreliable. In a gratuitous shot at Fremont Older, the court noted that his "activities on behalf of the bomb defendants had not always been commendable," whatever that may have meant. Evading the acquittals of Rena Mooney and Israel Weinberg, which destroyed the cases against Billings and Mooney, the court explained that Oxman was not called as a trial witness because he was himself under investigation and a defendant, "and the prosecution did not desire to be confronted with such collateral issues."

The decision was remarkable for what it left out. There was no mention of the arrests without warrants or the defendants being held incommunicado. No mention of Swanson's directing the arrests and prosecutions. Judge Griffin's request for a new trial after the Oxman letters wasn't mentioned. Other points "not discussed herein are lacking in merit and do not require further notice." And, of course, there was the usual dredging up of Mooney's background and radical beliefs.

As in 1930, Justice William Langdon was the dissenter: "The question here involved is not the guilt or innocence of Thomas J. Mooney...The preponderance of the material, credible evidence leads me to conclude that on his trial petitioner was not accorded due process of law. For that reason, the writ of *habeas corpus* should issue."

The defense had just one more recourse: asking the United States Supreme Court to review the decision of the California Supreme Court. Davis went to New York and was admitted to practice before the United States Supreme Court. In 1938, the defense filed a brief for *certiorari* (permission to appeal), which charged that the California Supreme Court had "become a party to the frame-ups...by its deliberate misrepresentations, distortions, suppressions and evasions of material evidence...[it] has itself been guilty of what is the moral equivalent of the prosecutor's knowing use of perjury and deliberate suppression of evidence."

Billings and Mooney returned to their respective prisons. Tom had developed gastrointestinal troubles during his long incarceration, and he perforated an ulcer, which almost killed him. There was a huge outcry: hasn't California done enough to this man? Mooney recovered. The state assembly passed a resolution favoring pardon, and in July 1937, twenty-five United States senators and eighty-six congressmen signed a letter to President Roosevelt demanding another federal investigation. In March 1938, Mooney addressed the California State Assembly. Although it was unclear if the legislature had the power to grant a pardon, a resolution by the Assembly to grant Mooney one passed, but it was tabled in the Senate. In Washington, the U.S. Supreme Court, put on the spot, denied the petition, Justices Hugo Black and Stanley Reed dissenting. Billings and Mooney had been in prison for more than twenty-two years, and the last available legal recourse on their behalf had failed.

1939

Free at Last

In California, Democratic senator Culbert Levy Olson was running a strong campaign for governor against Frank Merriam. Born in Fillmore, Utah, in 1876, Olson had Latter-Day Saints (Mormon) parents, but his mother at least was atypical, being an advocate of women's suffrage and Utah's first elected female official. Culbert Olson was also atypical, breaking with his parents' church at age ten and becoming an atheist. After studying law and journalism at Brigham Young University, Olson went to Washington, D.C., where he earned a law degree. Relocating to California in 1920, Olson was a Progressive Democrat and was elected in 1934 to the California Senate, where he enthusiastically supported Franklin Roosevelt's New Deal. Olson was Upton Sinclair's campaign manager in 1934, but unlike Sinclair, he was supported by Roosevelt, and George Davis was his campaign manager. Mooney had support from labor and agreed to endorse Olson in exchange for a promise of pardon (the deal was not made public). Olson defeated Merriam, becoming the first Democratic governor of California in the twentieth century. Merriam was a lame duck and could have pardoned Mooney in November 1938, but like his predecessors, he did nothing.

The night before Olson's inauguration, Davis heard rumors that Olson was considering delaying the pardon. He organized a delegation of labor leaders to call on Olson. Olson suggested a hearing on Mooney's pardon petition in his office for Saturday, January 7, 1939. Davis wanted the hearing held in an environment more congenial for press and film and arranged with groundskeeper Frank Killiam for the hearing to be held in the Assembly

Governor Culbert L. Olson, *left*, presents Tom Mooney, *right*, with a full and unconditional pardon as George Davis (mustache and glasses) looks on. *San Francisco Public Library History Room.*

chambers. The hearing was broadcast nationally and by short-wave radio. Early Saturday morning, Mooney, San Quentin warden Smith and Davis drove to Sacramento. Cora Older was driven up by young Alan Cranston, whose father, William, had commuted on the same train as Fremont Older and who was a frequent guest at the Olders' ranch. California had a new attorney general, Earl Warren, who had requested Olson to say nothing that

Twenty-two and a half years after Preparedness Day, Rena weeps at Tom's release. At left is Rena's sister, Mrs. Belle Hammerberg. *San Francisco Public Library History Room.*

would cast discredit on the legal procedures, but Olson disregarded Warren's advice, and as the whole country and much of the world listened, Olson said that he had no doubt that Mooney had been convicted on perjured testimony. In an atmosphere thick with emotion, Olson handed Mooney his unconditional pardon and declared him free.

The Mooneys saw Billings, whom Olson had taken care to mention at the hearing, in Folsom Prison, and they returned to San Francisco. On Sunday, January 8, Davis, the Mooneys and actor Melvyn Douglas and his wife, Helen Gahagan Douglas, drove from Sacramento to Berkeley and took the ferry to San Francisco. A parade, eerily reminiscent of the Preparedness parade twenty-two and a half years earlier, marched up Market Street to Civic Center, with Tom leading, followed by labor leaders Harry Bridges and Jack Shelley; George Davis; Rena Mooney; Rena's sister, Belle; Tom's brother, John; and Tom's sister, Anna. A huge crowd fell in behind. Addressing the

Tom Mooney leads the parade up Market Street on Sunday, January 8, 1939. Behind Mooney are Harry Bridges (second from left); Rena's sister, Belle; Rena; George Davis; Tom's siblings, Anna and John; and labor leader Jack Shelley. *Bancroft Library.*

Governor Culbert Olson commutes Billings's sentence as (left to right, standing) George Davis, Folsom Prison warden Plummer and Billings look on. *San Francisco Public Library History Room.*

crowd in Civic Center, Mooney said that it was the happiest day of his life and regretted only that his mother and Fremont Older could not be present.

With Mooney pardoned, Billings's incarceration was more ludicrous than ever. Olson had unfortunately become incapacitated the evening after pardoning Mooney, and Davis had to submit Billings's petition for pardon to the State Prison Advisory Board, which voted three to two against. Judge Dunne, still living, had bitterly denounced Olson's pardon of Mooney and telegrammed the board to say that Billings had had a fair trial and was guilty. Earl Warren, who had voted with the majority, said that he had been influenced by Dunne's communication. Davis sent the pardon petition back to the California Supreme Court, which in October reluctantly (and, it would seem, spitefully) granted only a commutation of sentence to time served. Billings was released a convicted felon, without rights of citizenship.

Epilogue

In France, *l'Affaire Dreyfus* continued to provoke bitter reactions after his return from prison and reinstatement in the army. Threatened with violence if he attended Emile Zola's funeral, he went anyway. When Zola's remains were transferred to the Panthéon, an honor reserved for French heroes, artists, authors and other notables, Dreyfus attended and was shot and wounded, not fatally, by a right-wing journalist. Dreyfus reentered the army during World War I and served with distinction. He died in 1935, aged seventy-five.

In 1984, the French sculptor "Tim" was commissioned to execute a sculpture depicting Dreyfus. Tim created a lanky figure of an officer at attention, holding up a broken sword. There was difficulty finding a suitable location. The École Militaire and École Polytechnique, both of which Dreyfus had attended, refused. The sculpture was first placed in the famous Jardin des Tuileries and then moved to the tiny Place Pierre-Lafue. In 2002, the sculpture was vandalized with yellow paint and anti-Semitic slogans, possibly just a random act or possibly an act of lingering hatred from the *Affaire*.

Unlike Dreyfus, Tom Mooney did not live to enjoy his freedom. His defense committees were $20,000 in debt, and he went on speaking tours to raise money, but his gastrointestinal troubles reappeared and he underwent four operations. He asked Rena for a divorce, which she refused, and when word got out, sympathy for Tom fell off, as George Davis had warned Tom it would.

As Fremont Older and others observed, Mooney was never a true labor leader. The egotism and single-mindedness that had sustained him through imprisonment were not compatible with leadership. Mooney had spent almost twenty-three years fighting for his innocence and his freedom. They were his reasons for being, and once they were granted, his reasons for being evaporated. By the summer of 1939, the world was occupied with other things: on September 1, Hitler invaded Poland; Mooney had become irrelevant. He spent the last eighteen months of his life in St. Luke's Hospital, San Francisco, and died on March 6, 1942. Rena Mooney died from a heart attack, alone in her apartment, in 1952.

Warren K. Billings made a much better adjustment. In prison, he became engaged by correspondence to one Josephine Rudolph. As Billings was a convicted felon in California, they could not marry in the state and eloped to Nevada. Billings was active in labor affairs after his release, and having learned the watchmaker's trade in Folsom Prison, he set up in business on Market Street. He was pardoned and restored to full citizenship by Governor Edmund G. ("Pat") Brown in December 1961. Billings had become a generous and forgiving man, without malice. In a 1967 letter to San Francisco resident Mrs. Julie Giacalone, he wrote:

> [L]*et me beg you not to be too hard on poor Tom* [Mooney]. *He wasn't nearly as bad as his enemies try to paint him. He did have his faults, like all the rest of us, for he was no more than human, but* [he] *did have the courage of his convictions and the courage to stand up and fight for what he believed in…One of the things that people on the outside cannot understand is the so-called "break" between Tom and* [me] *after he got out and I was still in. Frankly, there was never any intent upon my part to break with Tom but I felt that I had to win over the people in the A.F.L. Labor movement that Tom had alienated with his pamphlet "Labor Leaders Betray Tom Mooney"…*
>
> *As for his actions toward Rena, well, there was a reason for that too, although I can't say that I agreed with Tom's reasoning on that. After I got out George T. Davis and I made every effort we could to get Tom to change his mind and go back to living with Rena but he was "bull-headed" and wouldn't do it. Actually they had grown apart during his years in prison, which often happens to men who are kept in for many years…*
>
> *I work two days a week for Maiden Lane Jewelers, at 47 Maiden Lane* [the street where Billings had sprayed paint-removing acid on cars during the Preparedness parade]—*Tuesdays and Thursdays, usually from ten to four—and also work on watches and clocks at home here,*

> *making a specialty of repairing antiques…I closed my shop in September, 1958, and went on Social Insecurity—that's why I have to work.*

Billings's wife, Josephine, died of cancer early in 1972. Billings died in Redwood City, California, aged seventy-nine, on September 4 of the same year. The *New York Times* ran a prominent obituary under the headline, "Figure in '16 Coast Blast," which wasn't strictly accurate. Billings willed his body to the University of California–San Francisco Medical Center.

It is sometimes said that in Dreyfus's case, the system worked to free and reinstate him, which is questionable. In Billings-Mooney, the system most definitely did *not* work. George Davis said that it was not the legal process that freed Tom Mooney but politics. If Olson or a like-minded governor had been elected earlier, Mooney would have been freed. If Olson had never been elected, Billings and Mooney would have died in jail. "Justice delayed is justice denied": with both men in jail for twenty-three years on the basis of perjured testimony concocted by the incompetent Fickert, with Cunha's connivance, justice was manifestly delayed and denied.

The case had its villains, cowards and heroes. Its villains included Martin Swanson, who planted the scheme in Fickert's susceptible and less-than-astute mind; Fickert and Cunha, who saw McDonald's affidavit and suppressed it when it did not support their case, as well as sprang Oxman as a surprise "witness" knowing that his story couldn't be true; Oxman, whose reasons for lying on the witness stand were never made clear; and the other prosecution witnesses. Its cowards included the justices who, like Pilate, washed their hands of the business; and Governors Stephens, Richardson, Young, Rolph and Merriam. Its heroes included Fremont Older, who defied his publisher and upheld the finest traditions of journalism with his relentless campaign for Billings's and Mooney's release; the defense lawyers, from McNutt to Davis; Justice Langdon; and Governor Olson. If there is a lesson in the Billings-Mooney case, it is that a democratic society must never let the emotions of a physical threat jeopardize civil liberties. Policy made in a moment of national panic is usually bad policy. As is so often true, Abraham Lincoln said it best:

> *What constitutes the bulwark of our own liberty and independence? It is not our frowning battlements, our bristling sea coasts, our army and our navy. These are not our reliance against tyranny. All of those may be turned against us without making us weaker for the struggle. Our reliance is in the love of liberty which God has planted in us. Our defense is in the spirit*

> *which prizes liberty as the heritage of all men, in all lands everywhere. Destroy this spirit and you have planted the seeds of despotism at your own doors. Familiarize yourselves with the chains of bondage and you prepare your own limbs to wear them. Accustomed to trample on the rights of others, you have lost the genius of your own independence and become the fit subjects of the first cunning tyrant who rises among you.*

The United States, and the State of California, learned little at first from Billings-Mooney. In 1942, President Roosevelt signed the infamous Executive Order 9066, authorizing the "relocation"—actually, imprisonment without judge, jury or trial—of American citizens of Japanese ancestry away from the Pacific Coast after the United States declared war on the Empire of Japan after the bombing of Pearl Harbor. Some 120,000 men, women and children were ordered to leave their homes to be settled in high-desert camps, not because they had demonstrated either disloyalty to the United States or loyalty to the Japanese empire, but just because of who they were. It was a reiteration in principle of the prosecutions of Billings, Mooney and the other defendants, not because of evidence against them, but because of who they were. Individuals who had every reason to know better but acquiesced in "relocation" included Governor Culbert Olson.

Culbert Olson was defeated for reelection by Earl Warren in 1942, but not, apparently, because of his pardon of Mooney and release of Billings. As governor, Warren seemed no more concerned with civil liberties than he had been as attorney general, and he also acquiesced in "relocation." But Warren was one of the most popular Republican politicians of the twentieth century and the most popular governor in California's history, and he was appointed chief justice of the United States Supreme Court by President Eisenhower, possibly as a way of removing him from Republican politics.

As chief justice, Warren showed unexpected capacity for growth, which became evident when he wrote the unanimous decision in *Brown v. Board of Education*, declaring segregation in public schools unconstitutional. Citing the Fourteenth Amendment, as Davis had done earlier, the Warren Court rendered some of the most significant decisions in the field of civil liberties in American history: *Mapp v. Ohio*, which expanded the exclusionary rule to make evidence seized without a warrant inadmissible (Cunha, Fickert and others raided the defendants' premises with no warrant); *Gideon v. Wainwright*, which required states to provide an attorney to indigent defendants (Mooney was not allowed to see an attorney); and *Miranda v. Arizona*, which required police and prosecutors to inform a defendant of his or her right to silence and to have an attorney present (none of the defendants in 1916 were so informed). The rulings of the Warren Court made the perversions of the judicial process such as happened in the Billings-Mooney case unlikely ever to be repeated; let us hope.

Fremont Older's *Call-Bulletin* continued as a Hearst publication until the late 1950s, when it was purchased by the Scripps-Howard chain and merged with the evening *San Francisco News*. By 1965, when many newspapers nationally had either merged or gone out of business, the Hearst Corporation bought the *News-Call-Bulletin* and merged it with the *San Francisco Examiner*, which it converted to an evening paper, the *Examiner-News-Call-Bulletin*. The name being too unwieldy, the paper became just the *Examiner*. It continued in publication until the year 2000, when Hearst acquired the *Chronicle* from the heirs of the founding de Young brothers and had to sell the interest in the *Examiner* for antitrust reasons. The *Examiner* is now tabloid size, some kind of cross between a local newspaper and an advertising handout.

Cora Older continued to live at Woodhills until the mid-1960s, when she broke her hip in a fall, at more than ninety years old. After her death in 1968, the house deteriorated, and much of its furnishings disappeared. The Mid-Peninsula Open Space District (MROSD) acquired the Olders' property in the 1970s as an addition to its other scenic hiking and bicycling preserves. The house was scheduled for demolition, but local journalists Mort and Elaine Levine generously volunteered to restore it in exchange for permission to live there at a nominal rent. The house, now furnished and maintained much as it was when Fremont and Cora Older lived there, is just above the entrance to the Fremont Older Open Space Preserve above Cupertino, California. It is a private residence but open for tours once a year.

The Clock

Artifacts of the Billings-Mooney case remain. In 1940, Russian-born artist Anton Refrigier won a commission to paint a series of murals depicting San Francisco history in the Rincon Annex Post Office, now called Rincon Center. His series, which was controversial from its inception, includes a mural on Billings-Mooney in which Mooney writes in his San Quentin jail cell as perjured witnesses point to him.

The street clock—several pictures of which show the hands pointing to just before and just after 2:00 p.m. as the Mooneys watched the Preparedness parade from the Eilers Building roof, establishing their alibi—was manufactured

Detail of the mural by Anton Refrigier in Rincon Center. Tom Mooney writes in his cell as prosecution witnesses point to him. *Photo by author, July 2013.*

Plaque on the "Alibi Clock." *Photo by author, August 2013.*

The "Alibi Clock." Manufactured in Seattle in about 1915, it is now outside 316 Georgia Street, Vallejo, California. *Photo by author, August 2013.*

by the Joseph Mayer firm, Seattle. It stood in front of Burnett Brothers Jewelers, 938 Market Street, until July 1932, when Burnett Brothers went out of business. It was purchased by Simon's Jewelers, 320 George Street, Vallejo, California, and moved to a sidewalk outside its business. When Simon's closed in 1984, the City of Vallejo bought the clock and had it moved a few feet to outside 316 Georgia Street, where it was maintained by Brown's Jewelers. Brown's having recently closed, the clock is now maintained by the Public Works Department of the City of Vallejo. A beautiful timepiece, it still ticks away the minutes, just as it did on that fateful Saturday, July 22, 1916.

Bibliography

The Bancroft Library, University of California–Berkeley, holds the Thomas Mooney Papers, approximately seventy cartons. It also holds the Fremont Older Papers, seven cartons. The most significant other source is the History Room, San Francisco Public Library Main Branch.

Books and Journals

Bean, Walton. *Boss Ruef's San Francisco*. Berkeley: University of California Press, 1967.

Begley, Louis. *Why the Dreyfus Affair Matters*. New Haven, CT: Yale University Press, 2009.

Bruce, John. *Gaudy Century*. New York: Random House, 1948.

Davenport, Robert. "Fremont Older in San Francisco Journalism: A Partial Biography, 1856–1918." PhD dissertation, University of California–Los Angeles, 1969.

deFord, Miriam Allen. *They Were San Franciscans*. Caldwell, ID: Caxton Printers Ltd., 1947.

Duffus, Robert L. *The Tower of Jewels*. New York: W.W. Norton, 1960.

Fitch, John. "The San Francisco Bomb Cases." *The Survey*, July 7, 1917. Journal of the Charity Organization Society of the City of New York.

Fowle, Eleanor. *Cranston*. Los Angeles, CA: Jeremy P. Tarcher Inc., 1984

Frost, Richard. *The Mooney Case*. Redwood City, CA: Stanford University Press, 1968.

Gentry, Curt. *Frame-Up: The Incredible Case of Tom Mooney and Warren Billings*. New York: W.W. Norton, 1967.

Hart, James D. *A Companion to California*. New York: Oxford University Press, 1978.

Hopkins, Ernest Jerome. *What Happened in the Mooney Case*. New York: Brewer, Warren & Putnam, 1932.
Hunt, Henry T. *The Case of Thomas J. Mooney and Warren K. Billings: Abstract and Analysis of Record before Governor Young of California*. New York: National Mooney-Billings Committee, 1925.
McGloin, John S.J. *San Francisco: The Story of a City*. San Rafael, CA: Presidio Press, 1978.
McGurrin, James. *Bourke Cockran: A Free Lance in American Politics*. New York: Charles Scribner's Sons, 1948.
Mowry, George. *The California Progressives*. Chicago: Quadrangle Books, 1951.
Older, Cora. *The Diary of Cora Baggerly Older*. Local History Studies, Foothill Community College District. Cupertino, CA: De Anza College, 1971.
———. "The Story of a Reformer's Wife." *McClure's Magazine* (July 1909): 277–93.
Older, Fremont. "A Glimpse of the Battle." *Overland Monthly* 50, no. 6 (December 1907): 546–48.
———. "Growing Up." [San Francisco] *Call-Bulletin*, 1931.
———. *My Own Story*. Revised and enlarged ed. New York: Macmillan Company, 1926. Originally published by Call Publishing Company, 1918.
Pollack, Walter, Zechariah Chafee Jr. and Carl Stern. *The Mooney-Billings Report*. Suppressed document of the U.S. National Commission on Law Observance and Enforcement, 1931.
Rolle, Andrew F. *California: A History*. New York: Thomas Y. Cromwell Company, 1963.
Swanberg, W.A. *Citizen Hearst: A Biography of William Randolph Hearst*. New York: Bantam Books, 1971.
Symes, Lillian. "Our American Dreyfus Case." *Harper's Magazine* (May 1931).
Ward, Estolv. *The Gentle Dynamiter*. Palo Alto, CA: Ramparts Press, 1983.
Wells, Evelyn. *Fremont Older*. New York: Appleton-Century, 1936.
Woehlke, Walter. "The Mooney Case." *Sunset Magazine* (January–May 1919).
Worthen, James. *Governor James Rolph and the Great Depression in California*. Jefferson, NC: McFarland and Company, 2006.

Newspapers

[San Francisco] *Bulletin*, 1905–18.
[San Francisco] *Call*, 1918–29.
[San Francisco] *Call-Bulletin*, 1929–39.
San Francisco Chronicle, 1916–39.
San Francisco Examiner, 1916–39.
San Francisco News, 1939.

Index

A

American Civil Liberties Union (ACLU) 153, 159
American Dreyfus Case, the 9, 10, 153
American Federation of Labor (AFL) 9, 176
anarchism 35, 55, 78, 101, 102, 103, 115, 120, 133
Argonaut (San Francisco) 107
Atherton, Gertrude 14
Austria-Hungary 23
Austro-Hungarian empire 23

B

Barlow, Lillian 130
Barrett, John 38
Benjamin, Raymond 115
Berkman, Alexander 59, 76
Billings, Warren K. 8, 9, 10, 11, 36, 37, 38, 39, 42, 48, 49, 59, 60, 61, 62, 63, 65, 66, 69, 74, 107, 112, 136, 144, 145, 153, 176
Black Hand (terrorist group) 23
Bohannon, Morris 76
Brady, Matthew 100, 102, 134
Brennan, Charles 109, 112
Brennan, James 8, 15, 112, 136
Bridges, Harry 162, 171
Brown, Edmund G. "Pat" 176
Building Trades Council (San Francisco) 42, 46
Bulletin (San Francisco) 8, 9, 12, 14, 16, 17, 19, 24, 25, 27, 28, 29, 30, 32, 33, 35, 38, 39, 41, 42, 46, 47, 49, 51, 52, 55, 56, 57, 59, 60, 61, 62, 63, 64, 65, 69, 72, 73, 74, 84, 86, 87, 88, 90, 96, 97, 100, 101, 102, 105, 108, 110, 111, 112, 113, 114, 115, 116, 119, 123, 124, 125, 126, 127, 143
Bunner, Stephen 53, 58, 60, 65, 88
Burgess, William 89, 90
Burke, Michael 77
Burns, William 13

C

Calhoun, Patrick 14, 29, 39
California Supreme Court 121, 130, 143, 151, 164, 166, 167, 173
Call-Bulletin (San Francisco) 143, 145, 154, 179

Call (San Francisco) 42, 127, 128, 130, 132, 135, 136, 143
Carranza, Venustiano 26
Casement, Sir Roger 26
Castle, Albert 57
Chicago Federation of Labor 92, 107, 138, 151
Chronicle (San Francisco) 42, 46, 47, 59, 61, 63, 65, 73, 99, 115, 124, 153, 160, 179
Clarke, Robert M. 102
Clifton, John 49, 50, 59
Cobb, Charles 109
Cockran, W. Bourke 67, 76, 77, 78, 80, 82, 83, 84, 87, 88, 89, 97, 118, 119, 134
Coghlan, Nathan 109
Colburn, Frederick 54
Commercial Club (San Francisco) 31, 57
Cranston, Alan 170
Crothers, Robert A. "R.A." 12
Cullinan, Eustace 29
Cunha, Edward 61, 66, 77, 81, 82, 88, 89, 94, 95, 96, 97, 98, 99, 100, 102, 103, 118, 121, 130, 135, 138, 139, 145, 146, 166, 177, 178

D

Dam, F.H. 132
Darrow, Clarence 19, 159
Davis, George T. 53, 160, 161, 166, 169, 171, 175, 176, 177
De Caccia, Al 72, 73
Densmore, John B. 129
Densmore Report, the 123, 129, 130, 132, 133, 134, 153
Díaz, Porfirio 26
Dickson, Edward 16
Dingee, William 131, 132
Dorgan, "Tad" 12
Dreyfus Affair, the 9, 10
Dreyfus, Alfred 7, 8, 9, 10, 175, 177
Dreyfus, Mathieu 8
Dublin, Ireland 25
Duffus, Robert L. 12, 19, 25, 27, 30, 32, 33, 39, 49, 51, 52, 53, 54, 55, 57, 127
Dunbar, Stewart "Stu" 49, 52, 54
Dunne, Frank 14, 36, 49, 69, 104, 109, 110, 114, 121, 152, 173

E

Edeau, Mellie 70
Edeau, Sadie 85, 86, 109, 110
Eickhoff, Henry 75
Eilers Building 35, 48, 61, 64, 65, 78, 80, 86, 121, 138, 179
Einstein, Albert 156
Ellis, Claude 92, 99
Ely, Fred 33
Embarcadero, the 41
Ernst, Hugo 31
Esterhazy, Ferdinand 9
Examiner-News-Call-Bulletin (San Francisco) 179
Examiner (San Francisco) 26, 46, 47, 57, 59, 61, 63, 65, 66, 84, 90, 100, 101, 179

F

Fair, Charles 131
Fair, James 147
Fairmont Hotel (San Francisco) 98, 131
Ferdinand, Archduke Franz 23
Ferrari, Louis 103, 109, 110, 111, 114, 118, 121, 145
Ferry Building 40, 41, 47, 49, 66, 81, 86
Fickert, Charles M. 8, 15, 54, 88, 147
Field, Sara Bard 42, 45
Finerty, John 159
Fitch, John A. 102
Folsom Prison 38, 148
Ford, Blackie 35
Fox, Adam 51, 84
France 7, 9, 10, 23, 131, 156, 175

Francis, Charles 105, 120
Frankfurter, Felix 117, 134
Fremont Older Open Space Preserve 179
Furuseth, Andrew 96, 115, 142

G

Germany 7, 9, 23, 25, 29, 45, 47, 105, 156
Glasgow, Scotland 120
Glesson, Edgar "Scoop" 12, 49, 51, 52, 54, 129
Goff, Charles 58, 99, 128
Goldberg, Rube 12
Goldman, Emma 59, 101
Grady, Harry F. 31
graft prosecution 14, 15, 16, 29, 32, 44, 58, 96, 109, 110, 148
Griffin, Franklin 76, 87, 103, 110, 115, 134, 139, 141, 142, 143, 152, 154, 156, 157, 166, 167

H

Hague, The (Netherlands) 106, 120
Hamilton, Wade 48, 78
Hammerberg, Belle 89
Hand, Draper 58, 61, 77, 135, 136, 137, 151, 167
Hanlon, Charles 42, 116
Hannah, Archbishop Joseph 118
Hatcher, Earl 138
Haynes, Frank P. 115
Hearst, George 128
Hearst, Phoebe Apperson 26
Hearst, William Randolph 56, 124
Heney Francis J. 13, 14, 15, 16, 58, 109
Henshaw, Frederick 118, 130, 147
Hoffman, Carl 49, 51, 52
Hopkins, Ernest J. 12, 16, 28, 35, 49, 51, 52, 53, 54, 57, 58, 73, 74, 80, 153
Huerta, Victoriano 26
Hughes, Charles Evans 31, 163
Hurley, Edgar 37

I

International Workers Defense League (IWDL) 38, 95

J

Jackson, Reverend John M. 28
Johnson, Charles 50
Johnson, Hiram 16, 35, 76, 78, 105, 140
Jordan, David Starr 26, 42, 141
Judd, Norris 130
Judd, Virginia 130

K

Kellogg, F.W. 124, 127
Kent, William 115, 116, 118
Kerch, W.C. 75
Kidwell, Alice 70, 75
Kidwell, D.J. 75
Kimberlin, Elmer 50, 75
Klein, Nicholas 33
Knapp, Hetta 51
Koster, Frederick 30, 31
Kytka, Theodore 79, 97

L

Lanborn, Lea 58
Lane, Rose Wilder 12
Langdon, William 13, 149, 167
Lavin, Belle 61
Law and Order Committee (San Francisco) 31, 58, 67, 108, 124, 162
Lawlor, George 51
London, England 25, 26

M

Machinists' Union 48
MacNevin, William 77, 139, 152
Market Street 11, 14, 19, 35, 37, 41, 47, 48, 51, 52, 53, 54, 61, 70, 75, 82, 83, 84, 85, 91, 99, 103, 111, 112, 113, 135, 136, 148, 162, 171, 176, 181

Matheson, Duncan 51, 53, 58, 66, 99, 103, 137
McCarthy, P.H. 108
McDevitt, William 42
McDonald, John 50, 65, 70, 114, 136, 137, 144, 145, 147
McKenna, Reginald 25
McKenzie, Edwin 95, 98, 145
McKenzie, Harry 76
McNutt, Maxwell 38, 67, 68, 70, 71, 73, 75, 76, 78, 80, 88, 90, 91, 92, 95, 109, 118, 119, 121, 140, 166, 177
Merriam, Frank 161, 169
Mooney, Anna 162
Mooney, Bernard 33
Mooney, Mary 89, 151, 157, 162, 166
Mooney, Rena 34, 35, 36, 39, 40, 43, 48, 61, 62, 63, 64, 66, 80, 89, 91, 103, 104, 109, 110, 114, 118, 121, 130, 135, 138, 158, 165, 166, 167, 171, 175, 176
Mooney, Thomas J. (Tom) 8, 9, 10, 11, 33, 34, 35, 36, 37, 38, 39, 40, 42, 43, 48, 55, 61, 63, 64, 77, 81, 84, 88, 89, 90, 105, 106, 109, 110, 112, 118, 120, 138, 151, 153, 156, 157, 158, 162, 166, 167, 175, 176, 177
Mooney v. Holohan 163
Mulholland, Frank 91
Mullally, Thornwell 29, 42, 51

N

National Laborers Organization (Holland) 106
Nelson, Arthur 51
Nieto, Rabbi Jacob 42, 45, 57
Nockles, E.N. "Big Ed" 92, 107
Nolan, Edward 61, 66, 86
North End Police Station 61

O

Oakland, California 28, 30, 53, 57, 65, 70, 72, 85, 86, 89, 111, 112, 167
O'Connor, Thomas 95, 97, 98
Oelrichs, Theresa Fair 131
Older, Cora (Mrs. Fremont) 12, 19, 32, 38, 124, 126, 128, 147, 164, 170, 179
Older, Fremont 9, 10, 12, 13, 14, 15, 16, 17, 18, 19, 28, 29, 30, 32, 38, 39, 47, 49, 51, 55, 64, 90, 96, 98, 99, 100, 101, 104, 108, 109, 116, 120, 123, 126, 127, 136, 138, 140, 143, 147, 149, 151, 152, 153, 154, 156, 160, 162, 163, 167, 170, 173, 176, 177, 179
Olson, Culbert L. 169, 178
Oxman, Frank 81, 82, 83, 84, 85, 86, 88, 89, 90, 91, 92, 93, 94, 95, 96, 97, 98, 99, 100, 101, 102, 103, 104, 105, 107, 108, 109, 110, 111, 112, 114, 115, 118, 124, 134, 135, 136, 138, 139, 141, 142, 147, 152, 154, 156, 157, 158, 166, 167, 177
Oxman letters 94, 96, 97, 98, 101, 103, 105, 109, 110, 112, 115, 118, 124, 134, 147, 167

P

Pacific Coast Defense League 42
Pacific Gas & Electric Company (PG&E) 36, 37, 38, 61
Painter, George, MD 51
Palace Hotel (San Francisco) 53, 89, 94, 126, 132, 160
Panama-Pacific International Exposition (PPIE) 10, 20, 21, 39, 50
Parson, George 128
Patek, Dr. Robert 49
Pearse, Pádraic 25
Pendergast, M.T. 50, 65, 72
Pershing, John 26
Peterson, Walter 70, 112, 166, 167
Phelan, James 29

Pickering, Loring, Jr. 32, 123, 127
Powers, John 49
Preparedness 8, 10, 27, 28, 29, 32, 41, 42, 44, 45, 46, 57, 77, 78, 89, 94, 96, 100, 101, 104, 107, 108, 109, 110, 111, 115, 116, 121, 122, 135, 137, 143, 144, 149, 151, 157, 158, 160, 162, 166, 171, 176, 179
Preston, John 146

R

Richardson, Friend 139
Rigall, Edward 91, 92, 93, 94, 95, 97, 98, 99, 100, 108, 115, 142, 167
Rigall, Mrs. F.D. 92
Ripley, Robert 12
Rolph, James "Sunny Jim" 19, 20, 21, 51, 62, 63, 128, 135, 136, 150
Rominger, Louis 75
Roosevelt, Franklin 29, 163, 169
Roosevelt, Theodore 13, 30, 115
Rowell, Chester 16, 116, 140, 141
Ruef, Abraham 12, 13, 14, 16, 17, 18, 96, 149, 152
Russia 23, 24, 47, 105, 117, 120, 121

S

Sacramento, California 37, 38, 61, 69, 75, 104, 117, 138, 143, 164, 170, 171
Samuels, Samuel 109, 110
Sandburg, Carl 19
San Francisco Chamber of Commerce 31, 32
San Francisco Labor Council 38, 40, 46, 165
San Quentin Prison 17, 76, 90, 133, 151, 155, 158, 162, 170, 179
Sapiro, Aaron 151, 152
Schmitz, Eugene E. 12, 13, 14, 15
Seawell, Emmet 109, 110
Shaw, Addison 165
Shaw, George Bernard 45, 156
Shaw, Victor 121
Sheridan, Frank 74
Shortridge, Samuel 100, 115
Sinclair, Upton 140, 162, 169
Smith, Estelle 61, 62, 63, 70, 75, 76, 103, 109, 111, 136, 144, 145, 147, 148, 152, 156, 157
Smith, William 70, 111, 167
socialism 33, 34, 35, 78, 120, 162
Sooy, Charles H. 138
Spreckels, John 100
Spreckels, Rudolph 13, 28, 42, 44, 115, 116
Steffens, Lincoln 19, 156
Stephens, John 104
Stephens, William 105, 139
Steuart Street 47, 49, 50, 53, 55, 59, 65, 69, 70, 72, 73, 75, 79, 80, 81, 83, 85, 91, 112, 136, 138, 147, 148, 151, 158, 160, 166, 167
Stout, Thomas 89, 90
St. Petersburg (Petrograd), Russia 105, 106, 120
Suhr, Herman 35, 36
Sullivan, Matt 152
Survey, The 17, 31, 102
Swanson, Martin 37, 39, 42, 43, 58, 60, 67, 73, 117, 118, 135, 177
Sweigert, Charles 115, 116, 117
Symes, Lillian 147, 153

T

Taylor, William 65, 75

U

Ulyanov, Vladimir Ilyich "Lenin" 35, 105, 120
Union Labor Party (ULP) 12
United Railways (URR) 14, 39, 40, 42, 44, 61, 64
United States Supreme Court 163, 165, 167, 178

V

Van Loo, Mrs. Kingsley 57
Villa, Francisco "Pancho" 26, 36

W

Walker, James "Jimmy" 151
Walsh, Frank 137, 142, 151, 159
Warren, Earl 170, 178
Washington, George 23
Waste, William 165, 166
Watson, Major W.J. 50
Webb, Ulysses 100, 157
Webster, Daniel 87, 88, 90
Weeks, Samuel 49
Wells, Evelyn 90, 143
Wheatland Ranch 35
White, Chief of Police 47, 58, 60, 63
Wickersham Report, the 153, 159
Wilshire's Monthly 34
Wilson, William 117
Wilson, Woodrow 26, 78, 105, 117, 119, 120, 127, 133, 141, 153
Woodhills 18, 19, 32, 164, 179
World War I 23, 27, 105, 129, 140, 175

Y

Young, Clement Calhoun "C.C." 140, 151

Z

Zemansky, Harry 117
Zola, Emile 9, 175

About the Author

John Ralston is a third-generation San Franciscan. After receiving a degree in history from the University of California–Berkeley, he studied for a teaching credential at San Francisco State University. Taking a course in California history, the interest he had always had in his native city was rekindled by Professor Walton Bean's *Boss Ruef's San Francisco*. He has conducted research on the history of San Francisco and California ever since, acquiring books, articles and ephemera. He is a member of several local historical organizations and is program director of the Los Altos Hills Historical Society (LAHHS). He also writes for publication. This is his latest work.

Visit us at
www.historypress.net

This title is also available as an e-book